Scott Foresman

WITHDRAWN

Scott Foresman

Editorial Offices: Glenview, Illinois • Parsippany, New Jersey • New York, New York
Sales Offices: Parsippany, New Jersey • Duluth, Georgia • Glenview, Illinois
Coppell, Texas • Ontario, California

Credits

Illustrations

Elizabeth Allen: pp. 38, 39, 40, 47, 51, 52, 53, 54, 55, 56, 67, 69, 70, 71, 72; **Bill Basso:** p. 2; **Joe Boddy:** pp. 9, 10, 11, 15, 25, 26, 27, 41, 42, 43; **Penny Carter:** pp. 135, 141, 145; **Bill Colorus:** pp. 167, 168, 170, 172, 199, 200; **Mena Dolobowsky:** pp. 122, 125, 126, 133, 134, 137, 138, 139, 140, 141, 152, 153, 154, 227, 237, 238, 240, 243, 244; **Eldon Doty:** pp. 68, 87, 92, 93, 94, 97, 107, 116, 132, 182; **Ruth J. Flanagan:** pp. 12, 28, 60, 82, 110, 126, 142, 164, 176, 192, 208, 246; **Tom Garcia:** pp. 148, 214; **Jerry Gonzales:** p. 84; **Susan Hall:** pp. 3, 4, 5, 6, 7, 8, 19, 20, 21, 22, 23, 24, 35, 36, 37, 48, 57, 58, 59, 63, 64, 73, 75, 76, 79, 80, 81, 155, 157, 158, 161, 163, 245; **Olga Jakim:** p. 66; **Patrick Merrell:** pp. 85, 86, 88, 89, 90, 101, 102, 103, 104, 105, 106, 117, 118, 119, 120, 121, 129, 130; **John Nez:** p. 18; **Melanie Reim:** pp. 50, 100, 198; **Doug Roy:** pp. 201, 202, 204, 215, 216, 217, 219, 220, 231, 232, 233, 235, 236; **Joanna Roy:** pp. 34, 166, 230; **John Sanford:** cover; **Jessica W. Stanley:** pp. 174, 175, 176, 180, 183, 184, 185, 186, 187, 188, 189, 190, 191, 195, 196, 205, 206, 207, 211, 221; **George Ulrich:** pp. 109, 113

CURR
LB
1573
.S38
2004
gr.2
unit 4-6
practice

WITHDRAWN

ISBN: 0-328-02245-4
ISBN: 0-328-04049-5

Copyright © Pearson Education, Inc.

All Rights Reserved. Printed in the United States of America. The blackline masters in this publication are designed for use with appropriate equipment to reproduce copies for classroom use only. Scott Foresman grants permission to classroom teachers to reproduce from these masters.

8 9 10 V011 10 09 08 07 06 05 04
7 8 9 10 V011 10 09 08 07 06 05 04

Table of Contents

Unit 5

All Aboard!

	Family Times	Phonics	High-Frequency Words	Comprehension	Grammar	Vocabulary	Research and Study Skills	Phonics Review	Spelling	Selection Test	Writing Process
Space Dreams Man on the Moon	83-84	85-86	87	88	89, 94	90	91	92, 97	93, 98	95-96	
Two Lunches at the Mill Going to Town	99-100	101-102	103	104	105, 109	106		107, 113	108, 114	111-112	
A True Boating Family Riding the Ferry with Captain Cruz	115-116	117-118	119	120	121, 125	122		123, 129	124, 130	127-128	
Splash! Down in the Sea: The Jellyfish	131-132	133-134	135	136	137, 141	138		139, 145	140, 146	143-144	
Tex and the Big Bad T. Rex Let's Go Dinosaur Tracking!	147-148	149-150	151	152	153, 158	154		155, 161	156, 162	159-160	157, 163

Unit 6

Just Imagine!

	Family Times	Phonics	High-Frequency Words	Comprehension	Grammar	Vocabulary	Research and Study Skills	Phonics Review	Spelling	Selection Test	Writing Process
The Clubhouse Lemonade for Sale	165-166	167-168	169	170	171, 176	172	173	174, 179	175, 180	177-178	
Start Collecting! It's Fun! The Puddle Pail	181-182	183-184	185	186	187, 191	188		189, 195	190, 196	193-194	
Stone Soup: A Folktale Stone Soup	197-198	199-200	201	202	203, 207	204		205, 211	206, 212	209-210	
A Good Idea Annie's Gifts	213-214	215-216	217	218	219, 223	220		221, 227	222, 228	225-226	
Wicker School Takes Action City Green	229-230	231-232	233	234	235, 240	236		237, 243	238, 244	241-242	239, 245

Family Times

Hear the Cheers

The Great Ball Game

It Happens Once a Year

Our family game is almost here.
My family comes from far and near.
They bring their bats. They bring their gear.
It happens once a year.

Suddenly, dreary clouds appear.
But it will clear. We have no fear!
Our family game is almost here.
It happens once a year.

The clouds are gone. The sky is clear.
We start to play. We start to cheer.
Our family game is finally here.
It happens once a year.

This rhyme includes words your child is working with in school: words with *eer* and *ear* where the letter *r* changes the vowel sound (*cheer, near*) and words with the suffix *-ly* (*suddenly, finally*). Sing "It Happens Once a Year" together. Clap when you hear a word that rhymes with *year.*

(fold here)

Name: _____

© Scott Foresman 2

You are your child's first and best teacher!

Here are ways to help your child practice skills while having fun!

Day 1 Work with your child to make up a silly poem using as many words as you can that rhyme with *deer* and *year.*

Day 2 Write these words on index cards: *ago, better, head, idea,* and *still.* Take turns picking a card and giving a clue about the word for the other players to guess.

Day 3 After shopping for food together, point out to your child how your food storage is organized. Then, have your child help with sorting and putting the groceries away.

Day 4 Read a story with your child. Ask your child to point out clue words that tell when something happened, such as *long ago, first, then,* or *finally.*

Day 5 Your child is learning to use adjectives that describe number (*two*), size (*large*), and shape (*round*). Point out different household objects and ask your child to describe their number, size, and shape.

Read with your child EVERY DAY!

Lift and Spell

Materials 20 buttons per player

Game Directions

1. Cover each of the words on the gameboard with a button.

2. Players take turns lifting a button off one word.

3. A player must add -ly to that word and spell the new word correctly to keep the button. If incorrect, the player returns the button.

4. When all the buttons have been lifted, the player with the most buttons wins!

Finish

slow	happy	sure	sudden
glad	sweet	nice	love
near	clean	angry	soft
short	swift	quick	loud
brave	kind	sharp	hungry

Name _____

Circle a word to finish each sentence.
Write the word on the line.

 y**ear**   st**eer**

1. Did you _____ ?

        hear

        heart

2. It was a singing _____ !

        dare

        deer

3. He sat very _____ to us.

        near

        next

4. I had no _____ .

        fair

        fear

5. It was _____ that he was friendly.

        clear

        close

 Notes for Home: Your child read and wrote words with *ear* and *eer,* such as *year* and *steer.* **Home Activity:** Ask your child to write a silly poem with words that rhyme with *year* and *steer.* Challenge your child to use as many *ear* and *eer* words as possible.

© Scott Foresman 2

Name _____

Add -ly to each word.
Write the new word on the line.

happily

---

1. lucky _____

2. quick _____

3. loud _____

4. near _____

5. slow _____

6. final _____

7. sure _____

8. soft _____

Draw a picture of an animal that moves slowly and one that moves quickly.

9. slowly

10. quickly

Notes for Home: Your child has learned to form words with the suffix -ly. **Home Activity:** Help your child make a list of words with the suffix -ly. Work together to use these words in sentences.

© Scott Foresman 2

Name _____

Pick a word from the box to finish each sentence.
Write the word on the line.

| ago | better | head | idea | still |

_____

1. A long time _____ there were two cold bears.

_____

2. One bear had a good _____ .

_____

3. He put a hat on his _____ .

_____

4. But he was _____ cold.

_____

5. His friend had a _____ idea.
   She used two hats!

Notes for Home: This week your child is learning to read the words *ago, better, head, idea,* and *still.* ***Home Activity:*** Make up a story together that begins: *A long time ago . . .* Use the words from the box in your story.

© Scott Foresman 2

Name _____

Look at the words and pictures.
Write each sport on the correct line.

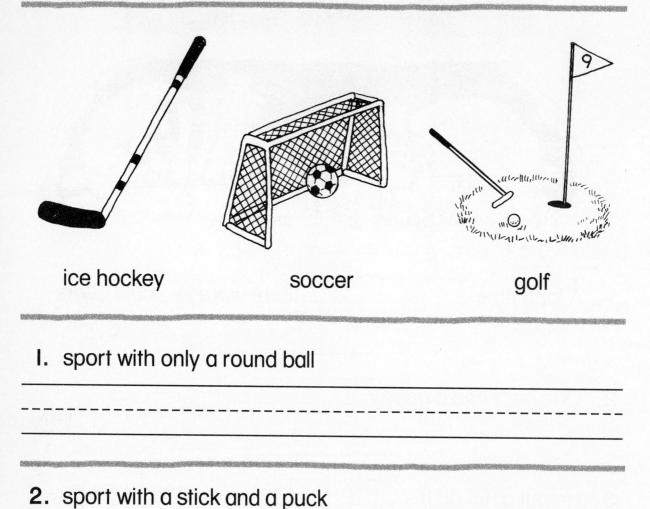

ice hockey   soccer   golf

1. sport with only a round ball

_____

- -

_____

2. sport with a stick and a puck

_____

- -

_____

3. sport with a stick and a round ball

_____

- -

_____

Notes for Home: Your child learned to classify objects. **Home Activity:** Invite your child to help you sort clean laundry. Discuss all the ways the laundry could be sorted, i.e., pattern, size, color, who it belongs to, kind of clothing (socks, shirts, and so on).

© Scott Foresman 2

Name _____

An **adjective** describes a noun.
An adjective may tell how many,
what size, or what shape.

Two bears play ball.
A **small** bat flies by.
The ball is **round.**

Circle the adjective in each sentence.
Draw a line from each sentence to the picture it matches.

1. There is one boy walking.

2. The clock is round.

3. I see a big bear.

4. I have three balls.

5. She has a square flag.

6.

7.

8.

9.

10.

Notes for Home: Your child identified adjectives that show number, size, and shape.
Home Activity: Play an I-Spy game with your child. Take turns picking something in the
room and giving the other person clues that describe number, size, or shape.

Level 2.2

Grammar: Adjectives **7**

© Scott Foresman 2

Name _____

Pick a word from the box to match each clue.
Write the word in the puzzles. The circled letters spell two words.

| ago | better | creature | head | lose | still | team |

1. sounds like *hill*

2. where your eyes and ears are

3. not worse

4. a long, long time _____

5. animal

6. a group of people playing together

7. not win

Notes for Home: Your child solved puzzles using new vocabulary words. *Home Activity:* Read the vocabulary words on this page aloud. Ask your child to write a story using these words.

© Scott Foresman 2

He co**u**ldn't reach the b**oo**ks.

Circle the word for each picture.

1.	2.	3.	4.
hood hide	hook hike	shore should	shook sock

5.	6.	7.	8.
crook creak	cork cook	could cold	fold foot

Find the word that has the same vowel sound as the picture.
Mark the space to show your answer.

9. ⬭ won
   ⬭ would
   ⬭ world

10. ⬭ took
    ⬭ top
    ⬭ too

© Scott Foresman 2

Notes for Home: Your child reviewed words with *oo* and *ou* that have the same vowel sound heard in *couldn't* and *books*. **Home Activity:** Ask your child to tell you about things he or she could do, using words with this vowel sound. (*I could look at a book.*)

bravely   friendly   lightly   slowly   softly   weekly

Add -ly to each word below to make a word from the box.
Write the new word on the line.

1. light

_____

_ _ _ _ _ _ _ _ _ _ _ _ _ _ _

_____

2. week

_____

_ _ _ _ _ _ _ _ _ _ _ _ _ _ _

_____

3. soft

_____

_ _ _ _ _ _ _ _ _ _ _ _ _ _ _

_____

4. brave

_____

_ _ _ _ _ _ _ _ _ _ _ _ _ _ _

_____

5. slow

_____

_ _ _ _ _ _ _ _ _ _ _ _ _ _ _

_____

6. friend

_____

_ _ _ _ _ _ _ _ _ _ _ _ _ _ _

_____

Pick a word from the box to finish each sentence.
Write the word on the line.

ago   head

_____

_ _ _ _ _ _ _ _ _ _ _ _ _

7. We had a contest two days _____ .

_____

_ _ _ _ _ _ _ _ _ _ _ _ _

8. I raced with a book on my _____ .

Notes for Home: Your child spelled words that end with *-ly* and two frequently used words: *ago, head.* **Home Activity:** Say each spelling word, then use it in a sentence. Invite your child to act out the sentence.

© Scott Foresman 2

Name _____

Pick an adjective from the box to finish each sentence.
Write the adjective on the line. Use each word only once.

| best | great | many | round | tall |

1. We are playing a _____ game.

2. We try to kick a _____ ball into the net.

3. Our team has two _____ players.

4. We score _____ goals.

5. Soccer is the _____ sport.

Notes for Home: Your child completed sentences using adjectives for number, size, and shape. **Home Activity:** Take turns describing an object in a room using adjectives. The other player tries to guess the object being described.

© Scott Foresman 2

Test-Taking Tips

1. Write your name on the test.

2. Read each question twice.

3. Read all the answer choices for the question.

4. Mark your answer carefully.

5. Check your answer.

© Scott Foresman 2

Part 1: Vocabulary

Find the word that best fits in each sentence.
Mark the space for your answer.

1. It is time for lunch, but Meg is _____ sleeping.
   ⊂⊃ still   ⊂⊃ between   ⊂⊃ across

2. The dinosaurs lived a long time _____ .
   ⊂⊃ tomorrow   ⊂⊃ quite   ⊂⊃ ago

3. Jed will _____ the game.
   ⊂⊃ climb   ⊂⊃ lose   ⊂⊃ peel

4. The ant is a tiny _____ .
   ⊂⊃ surface   ⊂⊃ creature   ⊂⊃ picture

5. Put a hat on your _____ !
   ⊂⊃ city   ⊂⊃ team   ⊂⊃ head

© Scott Foresman 2

GO ON ➡

Part 2: Comprehension

Read each question.
Mark the space for your answer.

6. The Birds and Animals have a —
   - ⬭ ball game.
   - ⬭ card game.
   - ⬭ jumping game.

7. Which one belongs on the same team as a dog?
   - ⬭ Fox
   - ⬭ Crane
   - ⬭ Hawk

8. How is Bat **not** like all the others?
   - ⬭ He has wings and teeth.
   - ⬭ He plays in the game.
   - ⬭ He can fly.

9. Who takes the ball from Crane at the end of the game?
   - ⬭ Bear
   - ⬭ Hawk
   - ⬭ Bat

10. You can tell from this story that bats do not —
    - ⬭ come out at night.
    - ⬭ fly south for the winter.
    - ⬭ use their wings much.

STOP

© Scott Foresman 2

Name _____

big   bigg**er**   bigg**est**

Circle a word in ( ) to finish each sentence.

1. The football is (bigger / biggest) than the baseball.

2. The basketball is the (larger / largest) ball.

3. The baseball is the (smaller / smallest).

4. The (heavier / heaviest) ball is the bowling ball.

5. Jan is (taller / tallest) than Bill.

6. Jill is the (faster / fastest) runner of all.

7. Bill is (slower / slowest) than Jill.

8. Is Bill (quicker / quickest) than Jan?

Find the word that you could use to compare three things.
Mark the space to show your answer.

9. ⬭ wet
   ⬭ wetter
   ⬭ wettest

10. ⬭ loud
    ⬭ louder
    ⬭ loudest

Notes for Home: Your child reviewed words with the comparative endings *-er* and *-est,* such as *bigger* and *biggest.* **Home Activity:** Help your child write a story about bigger animals helping smaller animals play a game, using comparative *-er* and *-est* words.

© Scott Foresman 2

| bravely | friendly | lightly | slowly | softly | weekly |

Pick a word from the box to match each clue.
Write the word on the line.

1. every seven days

_____
\- \- \- \- \- \- \- \- \- \- \- \-
_____

2. without fear

_____
\- \- \- \- \- \- \- \- \- \- \- \-
_____

3. not loudly

_____
\- \- \- \- \- \- \- \- \- \- \- \-
_____

4. not fast

_____
\- \- \- \- \- \- \- \- \- \- \- \-
_____

5. nice

_____
\- \- \- \- \- \- \- \- \- \- \- \-
_____

6. with a light touch

_____
\- \- \- \- \- \- \- \- \- \- \- \-
_____

Pick a word from the box to match each clue.
Write the word in the puzzle.

| ago | head |

7. It is on top of your body.
8. It means "in the past."

Notes for Home: Your child spelled words ending with *-ly* and two frequently used words: *ago, head*. **Home Activity:** Have your child look through a newspaper and list words with *-ly* endings. Help your child figure out what each word means.

© Scott Foresman 2

Family Times

Birthday Joy
The Best Older Sister

Join the Party

Join the party. It's for Roy.
Everybody bring a toy.

Let's sing songs and make some noise.
Let's play games that Roy enjoys.

Roy will make the hard-boiled eggs,
And flavorful foods like chicken legs.

Roy's mom Joy will mix and bake,
Colorful cookies and a big, round cake.

There's fun for every girl and boy.
Join the party. It's for Roy.

This rhyme includes words your child is working with in school: words with *oi* and *oy* (*Join, Roy*) and words with the suffix *-ful* (*flavorful, colorful*). Read aloud "Join the Party" with your child. Work together to write another verse for the rhyme.

(fold here)

Name: _____

© Scott Foresman 2

You are your child's first and best teacher!

Here are ways to help your child practice skills while having fun!

Day 1 Work with your child to write an advertisement that uses words that end with *-ful*, such as *beautiful* and *wonderful*.

Day 2 Have your child draw a picture of a father and his child. Then write a sentence about the picture using words your child is learning to read: *about, different, father, important, told.*

Day 3 Read a fairy tale or folk tale to your child. Then ask your child what lesson the story might teach and how the story is like something in his or her own life.

Day 4 Describe different objects by telling how they look, feel, smell, taste, or what sounds they make. See if your child can name the objects you describe.

Day 5 Your child is learning to write a personal narrative. Ask your child to write a letter to a friend or relative telling about something he or she did that day.

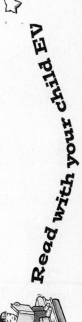

Read with your child EV___!

4

Spell the Word

Materials index cards, 1 button per player

Game Directions

1. Copy each word shown below on index cards.

2. Take turns drawing and reading a card aloud.
The other player must spell that word correctly.

3. If the player spells the word correctly, he or she
moves his or her button one space.

4. The first player to reach the end wins!

toy	ton	noise	royal
paint	toil	pail	point
boys	joined	foil	nose
coins	boiling	daily	coil
oil	joyful	soil	enjoy

Start

End

Circle a word to finish each sentence.
Write the word on the line.

 b<u>oi</u>l

cans   coins
_____

1. I have three _____ .

toy   tab
_____

2. I wanted a new _____ .

planted   pointed
_____

3. I _____ at it.

noise   nuts
_____

4. It makes lots of _____ .

job   joy
_____

5. It brings lots of _____ .

Notes for Home: Your child practiced using words with *oi* and *oy,* such as *coin* and *joy.* **Home Activity:** Work with your child to list other words with *oi* and *oy* that have the same vowel sound as *coin* and *joy.*

© Scott Foresman 2

Add -ful to each word in ( ).
Write the word on the line to finish each sentence.

help + -ful = help**ful**

_____
- - - - - - - - - - - - - - - - - -
1. It was a _____ party.   (wonder)

_____
- - - - - - - - - - - - - - - - - -
2. The room looked _____ .   (joy)

_____
- - - - - - - - - - - - - - - - - -
3. The children were _____ .   (play)

_____
- - - - - - - - - - - - - - - - - -
4. The music was _____ .   (cheer)

_____
- - - - - - - - - - - - - - - - - -
5. It was _____ after the party.   (peace)

Notes for Home: Your child wrote words with the suffix -ful, such as helpful. **Home Activity:** Read a story with your child. Challenge your child to find words in the story that can have the suffix -ful added to them, such as care, help, and play (careful, helpful, playful).

© Scott Foresman 2

Name _____

Pick a word from the box to finish each sentence.
Write the word on the line.

| about | different | father | important | told |

_____

1. My _____ was born in Korea.

2. He has _____ me stories about Korea.

3. One is _____ a Korean boy like me.

4. Life there is a bit _____ from life here.

5. These stories are _____ to me.

Notes for Home: This week your child is learning to read the words *about, different, father, important,* and *told.* **Home Activity:** Encourage your child to write a story with a character who is a father, using as many of these words as possible.

© Scott Foresman 2

Name _____

Read each story. **Follow** the directions.

I have a birthday party every year. My family is all there.
My friends come too. There are games and cake.
It is a lot of fun.

1. Circle the sentence that tells the big idea of this story.

   My birthday party is always fun.

   I am growing up.

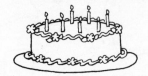

2. Underline the parts of the story that helped you tell
   the big idea.

I was going out to play, but my mom got sick. I had
to take care of my little brother. He can be a pest.
I know it is important to help out, so I didn't mind.

3. Circle the sentence that is the
   big idea of this story.

   Helping your family is important.

   A little brother can be a pest.

4. Underline the parts of the story that
   helped you tell the big idea.

 Notes for Home: Your child practiced finding the big idea in a story. **Home Activity:** Work with
your child to come up with an idea you both think is important, such as: *Always plan ahead.*
Help your child write about something that has happened in his or her life that conveys that idea.

© Scott Foresman 2

Name _____

An **adjective** describes a noun.
An adjective can tell how something looks, sounds, tastes, feels, or smells.

Apples taste **sweet**.

Circle the adjective in each sentence.
Draw a line from each adjective to the sense it goes with.

1. The ball looks red.

2. The soap smells fruity.

3. The tree bark feels rough.

4. The music sounds loud.

5. The stew tastes salty.

6.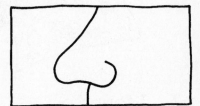

7.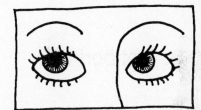

8.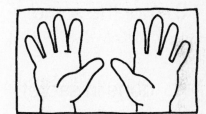

9.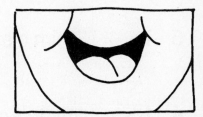

10.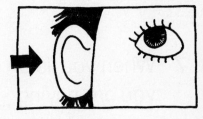

Notes for Home: Your child identified adjectives that relate to the five senses.
Home Activity: At dinner, use adjectives to describe how different foods look, taste, feel, smell, and maybe even sound.

© Scott Foresman 2

Name _____

Pick a word from the box to match each clue.
Write the word on the line.

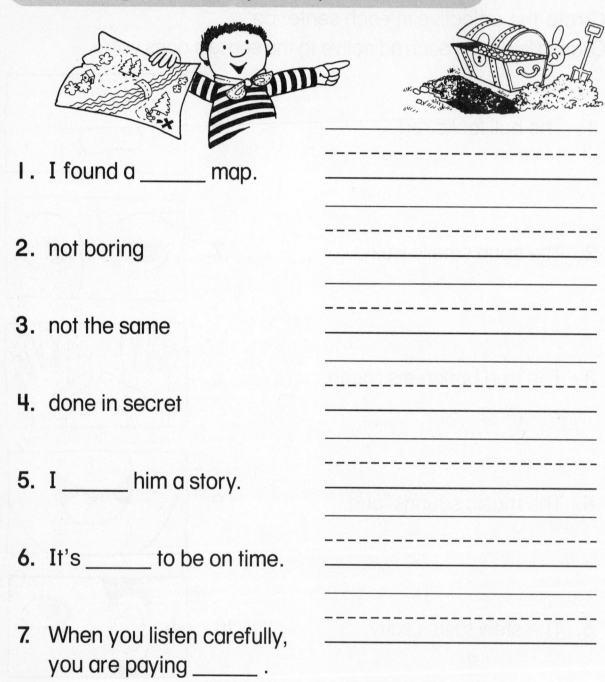

| attention | different | important |
| interesting | secretly | special | told |

1. I found a _____ map.

_____

2. not boring

_____

3. not the same

_____

4. done in secret

_____

5. I _____ him a story.

_____

6. It's _____ to be on time.

_____

7. When you listen carefully, you are paying _____ .

_____

Notes for Home: Your child used word clues to practice new vocabulary words.
Home Activity: Read the vocabulary words on this page aloud. Work with your child to use each word in a sentence.

© Scott Foresman 2

Level 2.2

Name _____

<u>ea</u>r

p<u>ee</u>ring

Circle the word for each picture.

1. spear   share

2. door   deer

3. rear   read

4. clear   corn

5. tires   tears

6. hear   hire

7. store   steer

8. fear   four

Find the word that has the same vowel sound as the picture.
Mark the space to show your answer.

9. ⬭ near
   ⬭ nail
   ⬭ snare

10. ⬭ yarn
    ⬭ yard
    ⬭ year

Notes for Home: Your child reviewed words with *eer* and *ear* in which the letter *r* changes the way a vowel sounds as in *ear* and *peering*. **Home Activity:** Help your child write a poem using rhyming words that have this vowel sound and these spellings.

© Scott Foresman 2

| boil | coin | point | spoil | voice | enjoy |

Write the word from the box that rhymes with each word below.

1. choice

_____

- - - - - - - - - - - - -

_____

2. toy

_____

- - - - - - - - - - - - -

_____

Write two words that rhyme with **foil**.

_____   _____

- - - - - - - - - - - -   - - - - - - - - - - - -

3. _____   4. _____

Pick a word from the box to match each clue.
Write the word on the line.

5. a penny

_____

- - - - - - - - - - - - -

_____

6. the end of a sharp pencil

_____

- - - - - - - - - - - - -

_____

Pick a word from the box to finish each sentence.
Write the word on the line.

father
told

_____

- - - - - - - - - - - - -

7. My _____ was born in China.

_____

- - - - - - - - - - - - -

8. He _____ me stories about it.

Notes for Home: Your child spelled words with *oy* and *oi,* such as *enjoy* and *coin,* and two frequently used words: *father, told.* **Home Activity:** Say each spelling word, and use it in a sentence. Repeat the word, and have your child write it.

© Scott Foresman 2

Name _____

Draw a line from each adjective to the sense it matches.

1. stinky

2. pretty

3. loud

4. warm

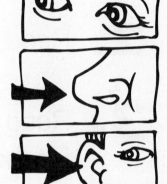

5. salty

Circle a word in ( ) to finish each sentence.

6. The apple looks (shut / shiny).

7. It smells (fair / fruity).

8. It tastes (sheet / sweet).

9. It feels (cold / code) in my mouth.

10. It makes a (card / crunchy) sound when I eat it.

Notes for Home: Your child identified adjectives that appeal to the five senses (sight, sound, taste, feel, and smell). **Home Activity:** When you eat or cook with your child, ask him or her to use adjectives to describe what each of the five senses can tell about the meal.

© Scott Foresman 2

Grammar: Adjectives and Our Senses **27**

Test-Taking Tips

1. Write your name on the test.

2. Read each question twice.

3. Read all the answer choices for the question.

4. Mark your answer carefully.

5. Check your answer.

© Scott Foresman 2

Part 1: Vocabulary

Find the word that best fits in each sentence.
Mark the space for your answer.

1. My birthday was a _____ day.
   - ⏗ guess
   - ⏗ next
   - ⏗ special

2. Amy feels it is _____ to help people.
   - ⏗ across
   - ⏗ important
   - ⏗ different

3. Babies need lots of _____ .
   - ⏗ attention
   - ⏗ creature
   - ⏗ thumb

4. We saw a very _____ show about ducklings.
   - ⏗ ago
   - ⏗ interesting
   - ⏗ secretly

5. Peggy _____ a funny joke.
   - ⏗ giggled
   - ⏗ lose
   - ⏗ told

GO ON ➡

Part 2: Comprehension

Read each question.
Mark the space for your answer.

6. After Kiju was born, Sunhi missed her time with —
   - ⬭ Robin.
   - ⬭ Halmoni.
   - ⬭ Jenny.

7. At first, Sunhi thinks that —
   - ⬭ everyone likes Kiju better than her.
   - ⬭ she is the best older sister.
   - ⬭ it would be great to have more babies.

8. Which sentence tells what this story is about?
   - ⬭ Sunhi told Halmoni about her day at school.
   - ⬭ Kiju always made such a mess.
   - ⬭ Everything changed for Sunhi when Kiju was born.

9. Why did Halmoni give Sunhi her surprise early?
   - ⬭ She could not keep it a secret.
   - ⬭ She wanted Sunhi to know that she loved her.
   - ⬭ She was afraid that Sunhi would find it.

10. In this story, Sunhi learned that —
    - ⬭ Halmoni is not her friend.
    - ⬭ it is better to be an only child.
    - ⬭ everyone is special.

STOP

© Scott Foresman 2

Name _____

Add -ly to each word below.
Write the new word on the line.
Hint: You will need to change **y** to **i** for some words.

1. lucky
_____
- - - - - - - - - - - - - - - -
_____

2. friend
_____
- - - - - - - - - - - - - - - -
_____

3. noisy
_____
- - - - - - - - - - - - - - - -
_____

4. happy
_____
- - - - - - - - - - - - - - - -
_____

5. loud
_____
- - - - - - - - - - - - - - - -
_____

6. final
_____
- - - - - - - - - - - - - - - -
_____

7. proud
_____
- - - - - - - - - - - - - - - -
_____

8. love
_____
- - - - - - - - - - - - - - - -
_____

Find the word where -ly has been added correctly.
Mark the space to show your answer.

9. brave
- ⊂⊃ bravely
- ⊂⊃ bravly
- ⊂⊃ bravelly

10. busy
- ⊂⊃ busyly
- ⊂⊃ busily
- ⊂⊃ busilly

Notes for Home: Your child reviewed words that have the suffix *-ly*. **Home Activity:** Words with *-ly* tell how an action is done. Name some action verbs *(run, sing)* and have your child use words with the suffix *-ly* to describe how each action could be done *(swiftly, sweetly)*.

© Scott Foresman 2

boil	coin	point	spoil	voice	enjoy

Pick a word from the box to match each clue.
Write the word on the line.

1. You'll find it at the end of a needle. _____

2. You use it to speak. _____

3. You do this to water to make tea. _____

4. You can use it to buy something. _____

5. It means "to be happy" with something. _____

6. It means "to become bad or rotten." _____

Change one letter in each word to make a word from the box.
Write the new word on the line.

father	told

7. gold _____

8. fatter _____

Notes for Home: Your child spelled words with *oi* and *oy,* such as *coin* and *enjoy,* and two frequently used words: *father, told.* **Home Activity:** Write each spelling word on a slip of paper. Take turns picking words and giving clues about each word for the other player to spell.

© Scott Foresman 2

Family Times

Treasure Pie

Bruno the Baker

The Bread Baker

I'll give you some bread, so you can be well fed.
And I'll spread it with butter and jam.
It's as light as a feather, and we'll eat it together.
And I'll serve you the bread with some ham.

Bread, bread, and more bread.
I'm a baker who spreads it with jam.
It's as light as a feather, and we'll eat it together.
I'm a very good baker. I am!

It's a pleasure to fix, all this bread I will mix.
And I'll use a bread timer to bake.
With my hat on my head, I will bake all the bread.
Then I'll make you a gingerbread cake.

Bread, bread, and more bread . . .

This rhyme includes words your child is working with in school: words with the short *e* sound spelled *ea* (*bread*) and words with the suffix *-er* (*baker*). Sing "The Bread Baker" together. Clap your hands for each short *e* word. Stamp your feet for each word that ends in *-er.*

(fold here)

Name: _____

© Scott Foresman   2

You are your child's first and best teacher!

Here are ways to help your child practice skills while having fun!

Day 1   Challenge your child to list as many words that end with the suffix *-er* as he or she can think of in one minute, such as *baker* and *helper.*

Day 2   Your child is learning to read these words: *large, ready, says, today,* and *wash.* Take turns giving each other a clue and naming the word that fits the clue, such as the clue *not yesterday* for the word *today.*

Day 3   Your child is learning about realistic stories and fantasies. Read a story or two with your child. Talk about whether the events in the story could really happen.

Day 4   Provide your child with a notebook or blank diary so he or she can start a journal at home. Encourage your child to write or draw in it every few days.

Day 5   Your child is learning to make announcements. Help your child create an announcement for a family event and have him or her present it to the family.

Read with your child EVERY DAY!

Short e Spelled ea

Materials 1 button per player, 1 coin

Game Directions

1. Players place both markers on Start and take turns flipping the coin. Move ahead one space for heads, and move two spaces for tails.

2. For each space landed on, players say a short e word spelled ea as in *bread*. Words must begin with the letter or letters shown in the space. Some possible answers are given below.

3. The first player to reach the end wins!

Answers: lead, leather, head, health, heavy, sweat, sweater, spread, breakfast, ready, weather, thread, dread

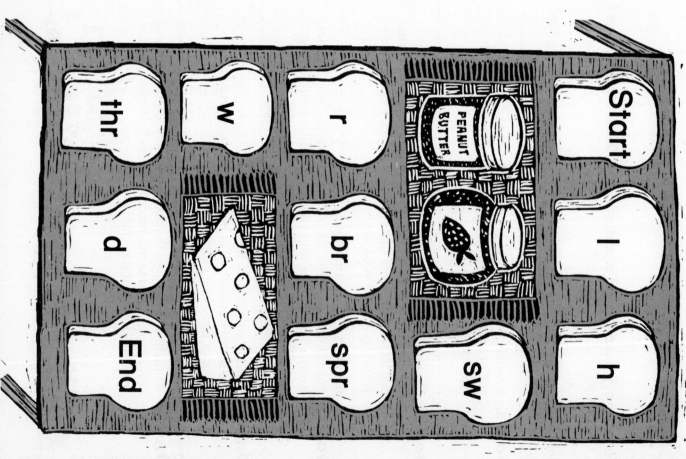

Name _____

Circle a word to finish each sentence.
Write the word on the line.

h<u>ea</u>d

read   rode

_____

1. I _____ a good book.

bread   braid

_____

2. It was about _____ .

healthful   helping

_____

3. Bread is _____ .

ready   reedy

_____

4. I'm _____ to eat!

spread   spare

_____

5. I _____ the jam.

 Notes for Home: Your child read and wrote words in which the short *e* sound is spelled *ea* as in *head*. **Home Activity:** Ask your child to write short rhyming sentences using words that rhyme with *head*.

© Scott Foresman 2

Name _____

Add -er to each word in ( ).
Write the word on the line to finish
each sentence.

run + -er = runn**er**

_____

(bake)
_____
– – – – – – – – – – – – – –
1. The _____ made bread.

(mix)
_____
– – – – – – – – – – – – – –
2. He used a _____ .

(time)
_____
– – – – – – – – – – – – – –
3. The _____ rang.

(help)
_____
– – – – – – – – – – – – – –
4. He gave it to his _____ .

(mark)
_____
– – – – – – – – – – – – – –
5. She wrote with a _____ .

Notes for Home: Your child wrote words that have the suffix *-er.* *Home Activity:* Work with
your child to make a list of words with the *-er* suffix. Ask your child to name the base word
for every word on the list. For example, *run* is the base word for *runner.*

© Scott Foresmany 2

Pick a word from the box to finish each sentence.
Write the word on the line.

| large | ready | says | today | wash |

_____
- - - - - - - - - - - - - - - -
1. We will bake a pie _____.

_____
- - - - - - - - - - - - - - - -
2. We _____ the apples.

_____
- - - - - - - - - - - - - - - -
3. We'll make a _____ pie.

_____
- - - - - - - - - - - - - - - -
4. Dad _____ it will take about an hour.

_____
- - - - - - - - - - - - - - - -
5. Now we are _____ to eat!

 Notes for Home: This week your child is learning to read the words *large, ready, says, today,* and *wash.* **Home Activity:** Work with your child to write a story about some food you like to make together. Use the words in the box in your story.

© Scott Foresman 2

Read each sentence.
Write Y if it tells something that could really happen.
Write N if it tells something that could not really happen.

------- 1. Jake has a dog.

------- 2. The dog says words to Jake.

------- 3. The dog plays with Jake.

------- 4. Jake walks to school with the dog.

------- 5. The dog reads stories to Jake.

Notes for Home: Your child identified whether a story event could really happen.
Home Activity: Ask your child to make up two stories, one realistic (can really happen)
and one a fantasy (includes events that can't really happen).

© Scott Foresmany 2

An **adjective** describes a noun.
Many adjectives come before the
nouns they describe.
Big is an adjective that describes **cake**.   He made a **big** cake.

Circle the adjective in each sentence.
Underline the noun it describes.

1. I smelled wonderful breads in the bakery.

2. I like the round loaves.

3. My mom bought long rolls.

4. She uses them to make huge sandwiches.

5. Her sandwiches are great!

Notes for Home: Your child has identified adjectives in sentences and the nouns they
describe. **Home Activity:** Name an object in your home. Ask your child to think of
adjectives to describe that object and use them in a sentence.

© Scott Foresman 2

Name _____

Pick a word from the box to match each clue.
Write the word on the line.

| kitchen | large | oven | present | ready | says | today | wash |

1.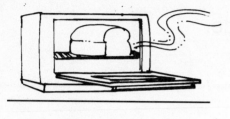

_ _ _ _ _ _ _ _ _ _ _ _ _ _ _ _

2. a room where you cook

_ _ _ _ _ _ _ _ _ _ _ _ _ _ _ _

3. It comes after yesterday.

_ _ _ _ _ _ _ _ _ _ _ _ _ _ _ _

4. big

_ _ _ _ _ _ _ _ _ _ _ _ _ _ _ _

5. You do this when you are dirty.

_ _ _ _ _ _ _ _ _ _ _ _ _ _ _ _

6.

_ _ _ _ _ _ _ _ _ _ _ _ _ _ _ _

7. Get _____.
Get set. Go!

_ _ _ _ _ _ _ _ _ _ _ _ _ _ _ _

8. talks

_ _ _ _ _ _ _ _ _ _ _ _ _ _ _ _

Notes for Home: Your child used word and picture clues to practice new vocabulary words.
Home Activity: Ask your child to choose several vocabulary words and use them to make up
simple riddles for you to solve, such as: *This is what I do when I take a bath.*

© Scott Foresman 2

c**oi**ns

t**oy**s

Circle the word for each picture.

1. bay   boy

2. sail   soil

3. point   paint

4. boil   bull

5. outer   oyster

6. nurse   noise

7. roll   royal

8. jet   joint

Find the word that has the same vowel sound as the picture.
Mark the space to show your answer.

9. ⬭ spoil
   ⬭ spoon
   ⬭ snail

10. ⬭ most
    ⬭ moist
    ⬭ moose

Notes for Home: Your child reviewed words spelled with *oi* and *oy* such as *coins* and *toys*.
Home Activity: Have your child use the words with *oi* and *oy* in sentences. Together, draw
pictures to go with the sentences.

© Scott Foresman 2

Name _____

| bread | breath | spread | sweat | thread | weather |

Pick a word from the box to match each picture.
Write the word on the line.

1.

2.

3.

_____

_____

_____

Pick a word from the box to match each clue.
Write the word on the line.

4. You hold this if you're under water. _____

5. You can do this with jam or butter. _____

6. You check this before going outside. _____

Pick a word from the box to finish each sentence.
Write the word on the line.

| ready | today |

7. _____ is Monday.

8. I'm getting _____ for school.

Notes for Home: Your child spelled words in which the short *e* sound is spelled *ea (bread)* and two frequently used words: *ready, today.* **Home Activity:** Help your child write new short *e* words by changing some letters in each spelling word, for example, *bread* becomes *break.*

© Scott Foresman 2

Circle the adjective or adjectives in each sentence.

1. Dad makes wonderful desserts.

2. He bakes many, tasty pies.

3. He only uses fresh, ripe fruit.

4. The pies taste sweet.

5. I like to eat pies when they are warm.

6. I once helped Dad make ten pies.

7. They were for a big party at my school.

Write a sentence on each line about something you eat.
Use at least one adjective from the box in each sentence.

| four | good | hot | red | round | small | sweet |

8. _____

9. _____

10. _____

Notes for Home: Your child identified adjectives in sentences and wrote sentences with adjectives. **Home Activity:** Have your child write a sentence using one adjective. Then, you repeat the sentence, adding a second adjective. Switch roles and repeat.

© Scott Foresman 2

Test-Taking Tips

1. Write your name on the test.

2. Read each question twice.

3. Read all the answer choices for the question.

4. Mark your answer carefully.

5. Check your answer.

© Scott Foresman 2

Part I: Vocabulary

Find the word that best fits in each sentence.
Mark the space for your answer.

I. Please _____ the dishes.
   ⊂⊃ follow   ⊂⊃ peel   ⊂⊃ wash

2. Are you _____ to go?
   ⊂⊃ high   ⊂⊃ ready   ⊂⊃ enough

3. That hat is too _____ for you.
   ⊂⊃ whole   ⊂⊃ large   ⊂⊃ still

4. Grandma is in the _____ baking a cake.
   ⊂⊃ oven   ⊂⊃ kitchen   ⊂⊃ present

5. We will go to school _____ .
   ⊂⊃ today   ⊂⊃ important   ⊂⊃ until

© Scott Foresman 2

GO ON ➤

Part 2: Comprehension

Read each question.
Mark the space for your answer.

6. Why do Bruno and Felix make a cake?
   - ⬭ Grandma tells them to make one.
   - ⬭ It is Bruno's birthday.
   - ⬭ Felix likes to mix the batter.

7. What does Bruno do first?
   - ⬭ He mixes the eggs.
   - ⬭ He turns on the oven.
   - ⬭ He puts some butter in a pan.

8. You can tell that Bruno and Felix —
   - ⬭ work well together.
   - ⬭ eat too much cake.
   - ⬭ don't like to read directions.

9. Why do Bruno's friends give him a new mixing bowl?
   - ⬭ His other bowl broke.
   - ⬭ They know he likes to bake.
   - ⬭ He needs a bowl to put flowers in.

10. Which part of the story could **not** really happen?
    - ⬭ A kitchen gets a little messy.
    - ⬭ Butter melts in a pan.
    - ⬭ Animals bake a cake.

STOP

© Scott Foresman 2

Add -ful to each word below.
Write the new word on the line.

a beauti**ful** cake

1. use

_____
- - - - - - - - - - -
_____

2. plenty

_____
- - - - - - - - - - -
_____

3. hope

_____
- - - - - - - - - - -
_____

4. color

_____
- - - - - - - - - - -
_____

5. help

_____
- - - - - - - - - - -
_____

6. peace

_____
- - - - - - - - - - -
_____

Find the base word for each word below.
Mark the space to show your answer.

7. careful
  - ⬭ car
  - ⬭ care
  - ⬭ caring

8. wonderful
  - ⬭ wonder
  - ⬭ won
  - ⬭ wand

Notes for Home: Your child reviewed words with the suffix *-ful*. **Home Activity:** Give your child some base words, such as *truth, pain, harm, fear, rest, cheer,* or *wonder.* Ask her or him to add *-ful* to each word and then use the new word in a sentence.

© Scott Foresman 2

| bread | breath | spread | sweat | thread | weather |

Pick words from the box to finish each sentence.
Write the words on the lines.

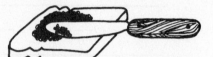

1.–2. I like to _____

jam on _____ .

3.–4. If the _____ is hot,

I _____ a lot.

5.–6. Hold your _____ Ned.

It will help you _____ .

Write the word from the box that rhymes with each word below.

| ready | today |

7. play

_____

8. steady

_____

Notes for Home: Your child spelled words in which the short *e* sound is spelled *ea* and two
frequently used words: *ready, today.* **Home Activity:** Ask your child to write a letter to a
friend or relative using as many of these spelling words as possible.

© Scott Foresman 2

Family Times

Paul Goes to the Ball

The Rooster

It's Family Time for All

Let's get together now.
It's family time for all.
My grandma makes some applesauce
As we play basketball.

Paul and Maude will climb
And even somersault.
My cousins walk and bounce a ball
While others drink their malts!

As day turns into night,
Mom knits or takes a walk.
The babies start to fall asleep.
Then we begin to talk.

This rhyme includes words your child is working with in school: words with the vowel sound heard in *Maude* and *ball* and words with silent consonants (*climb*). Sing the rhyme together. Then list all the words in the rhyme that have the same vowel sound heard in *Maude* and *ball*.

(fold here)

Name: _____

You are your child's first and best teacher!

Here are ways to help your child practice skills while having fun!

Day 1 Your child is learning to read words with *a*, *al*, and *au* that have the same vowel sound (*water, walk, sauce*). Work with your child to list words that rhyme with *walk* and *ball*.

Day 2 Work with your child to create a crossword puzzle or word search puzzle using words that your child is learning to read this week: *able, early, own, story,* and *thought.*

Day 3 Read a story with your child. Then ask your child to tell you what happened at the beginning, middle, and end of the story.

Day 4 Ask your child to name a favorite meal and provide details that support this opinion.

Day 5 Your child is learning about comparative and superlative adjectives (*bigger; biggest*). Ask your child to write an advertisement for a favorite game using adjectives that end in *-er* and *-est.*

Read with your child EVERY DAY!

© Scott Foresman 2

Silence Is Golden

Materials   paper, pencil, bag, 1 button

Game Directions

1. Write the words below on slips of paper and put them in a bag.

2. Players take turns picking a word from the bag and reading it aloud. Players must toss a button on the gameboard and land on the picture for that word to earn a point. If a player misses, the word is put back in the bag.

3. Play continues until each word has been used.

4. The player with the most points at the end of the game wins!

Words with Silent Consonants

comb, lamb, knife, knit, thumb, knot, climb, knee, doorknob

Circle the word for each picture.   ch<u>a</u>lk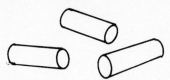

1. 	2. 	3. 	4. 
ball bell	walk wink	save sauce	well wall

5. 	6. 	7. 	8. 
tall talk	water wetter	tell tall	smell small

Draw a picture for each action.

9. falling

10. calling

© Scott Foresman 2

Notes for Home: Your child read words with the same vowel sound as *chalk* spelled *a, al,* and *au.* **Home Activity:** Together, name words that rhyme with *tall.*

Write **k** or **b** to finish each word.   <u>k</u>nee   lam<u>b</u>

1.

_____ nock

2.

com _____

3.

_____ nob

4.

_____ nit

5.

thum _____

6.

_____ not

7.

crum _____ s

8.

plum _____ er

 Notes for Home: Your child read and completed words with *kn* and *mb* that have silent consonants. **Home Activity:** Work with your child to write sentences using the *kn* and *mb* words on this page.

© Scott Foresman 2

Pick a word from the box to finish each sentence.
Write the word on the line.

> able   early   own   story   thought

1. Grandma told me a funny _____ .

2. She got ready for a party a day _____ .

3. She _____ it was on Saturday.

4. Luckily, she was _____ to go the next day.

5. It was easy because it was at her _____ house!

Notes for Home: This week your child is learning to read the words *able, early, own, story,*
and *thought.* **Home Activity:** Write these words on slips of paper. Ask your child to choose
slips at random, read each word aloud, and use it in a sentence.

© Scott Foresman 2

Write a number next to each sentence to show the right order.

1. On July 4, everybody came with food. _____

2. For weeks, our family planned a big picnic. _____

3. We ate the food and had a lot of fun. _____

4. He played a lot and got better and better. _____

5. John started to learn to play the piano. _____

6. John won the piano contest. _____

Notes for Home: Your child identified the order of story events. **Home Activity:** Ask your child to tell you the beginning, middle, and end of a story you have read together. Listen for your child to focus on important story events.

© Scott Foresman 2

Add -er to an adjective when you compare two nouns.

The striped balloon is **bigg<u>er</u>** than the dotted balloon.

Add -est when you compare more than two nouns.

The plain balloon is the **bigg<u>est</u>** balloon he has.

Circle a word to finish each sentence.

1. Bruno is the _____ child.   taller
                                                           tallest

2. This streamer is the _____ one of all.   longer
                                                           longest

3. This banner is _____ than last year's banner.   smaller
                                                           smallest

4. Kim is the _____ blower of balloons.   faster
                                                           fastest

5. The drum is _____ than the flute.   louder
                                                           loudest

Notes for Home: Your child has learned to use comparative and superlative adjectives.
Home Activity: When out with your child, point out two or more items in a group and ask
your child to compare the items.

© Scott Foresman 2

Pick a word from the box to match each clue.
Write the word on the line.

able   brook   early   feathers
growl   own   story

1. I'm _____ to ride a bike.

_____

2. not late

_____

3. Birds have these.

_____

4. It is often make-believe.

_____

5. to have something

_____

6. A bear makes this sound.

_____

7. a small stream

_____

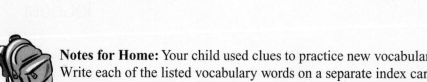

Notes for Home: Your child used clues to practice new vocabulary words. **Home Activity:**
Write each of the listed vocabulary words on a separate index card. Use the cards as flash
cards. Ask your child to read the word on each card and use it in a sentence.

© Scott Foresman 2

Name _____

Circle the word for each picture.   br**ea**kfast

1. head   heard

2. heavy   have

3. thread   three

4. leather   letter

5. father   feather

6. swap   sweat

7. bread   braid

8. speed   spread

Find the word that has the same **short e** sound as the picture.
Mark the space to show your answer.

9. ⬭ peach
   ⬭ weather
   ⬭ bean

10. ⬭ meeting
    ⬭ meaning
    ⬭ meadow

Notes for Home: Your child reviewed words in which the short *e* sound is spelled *ea*, as in *breakfast*. **Home Activity:** Ask your child to write a poem using words in which the short *e* sound is spelled *ea*.

© Scott Foresman 2

Name _____

climb   comb   lamb   kneel   knit   knot

Write three words from the box that begin with **kn**.

1. _____   2. _____   3. _____

Write three words from the box that end in **mb**.

4. _____   5. _____   6. _____

Pick a word from the box to match each picture.
Write the word on the line.

7.  _____

8. 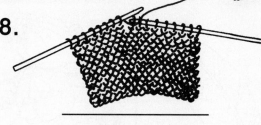 _____

Pick a word from the box to finish each sentence.
Write the word on the line.

story   able

9. Do you want me to read you a _____ ?

10. I am _____ to read it by myself!

 Notes for Home: Your child spelled words with silent consonants and two frequently used words: *story, able.* **Home Activity:** Say each spelling word, then use it in a sentence. Repeat the word, and have your child write it.

© Scott Foresman 2

Name _____

Circle an adjective to finish each sentence.

1. I went to the (bigger / biggest) party I've ever seen.

2. It was for Jack, the (older / oldest) of all the children.

3. I am six years (younger / youngest) than he is.

4. Jack was the (hungrier / hungriest) person at the party.

5. He ate the (larger / largest) piece of cake.

---

small   fast   hard

Add -er or **-est** to each word in the box.
Write a sentence using each new adjective.

6. _____

7. _____

8. _____

Notes for Home: Your child identified and wrote comparative and superlative adjectives that end with *-er* and *-est*. **Home Activity:** Ask your child to create an advertisement for a product, real or imaginary, using adjectives such as *brightest* or *bigger*.

© Scott Foresman 2

Test-Taking Tips

1. Write your name on the test.

2. Read each question twice.

3. Read all the answer choices for the question.

4. Mark your answer carefully.

5. Check your answer.

© Scott Foresman 2

Part 1: Vocabulary

Find the word that best fits in each sentence.
Mark the space for your answer.

1. He swims in the _____ .
   ⊂⊃ field ⊂⊃ brook ⊂⊃ feathers

2. Pat told us a long _____ .
   ⊂⊃ story ⊂⊃ able ⊂⊃ picture

3. The dog began to _____ .
   ⊂⊃ decide ⊂⊃ peel ⊂⊃ growl

4. Carlos got up _____ today.
   ⊂⊃ early ⊂⊃ between ⊂⊃ able

5. Liz has her _____ room.
   ⊂⊃ ripe ⊂⊃ own ⊂⊃ early

© Scott Foresman 2

GO ON

Part 2: Comprehension

Read each question.
Mark the space for your answer.

6. What did the rooster do first?
    - ⬭ He crowed at the sun.
    - ⬭ He got ready for the wedding.
    - ⬭ He asked the grass for help.

7. The rooster got his beak dirty when he —
    - ⬭ ate some corn.
    - ⬭ walked into the brook.
    - ⬭ ate the grass.

8. The rooster talked to the grass, the lamb, and the others because he —
    - ⬭ was a friendly bird.
    - ⬭ wanted them to go to the wedding.
    - ⬭ needed some help.

9. Which of these could really happen?
    - ⬭ A dog talks.
    - ⬭ A stick burns.
    - ⬭ The grass cries.

10. Why did everyone but the sun say no to the rooster?
    - ⬭ The rooster had not done anything for them.
    - ⬭ Everyone was too busy helping someone else.
    - ⬭ They did not want to be late for the wedding.

STOP

© Scott Foresman 2

Name _____

Add -er to each word below to make
a word that matches the picture.
Write the new word on the line.

bak**er**

1. time

_____

- - - - - - - - - - - -

2. sing

_____

- - - - - - - - - - - -

3. bat

_____

- - - - - - - - - - - -

4. farm

_____

- - - - - - - - - - - -

5. help

_____

- - - - - - - - - - - -

6. run

_____

- - - - - - - - - - - -

Find the word where the final **e** was dropped
before **-er** was added.
Mark the space to show your answer.

7. ⬭ diner
   ⬭ worker
   ⬭ drummer

8. ⬭ skater
   ⬭ cleaner
   ⬭ jogger

 Notes for Home: Your child wrote words that end with *-er*. **Home Activity:** Ask your child to make a list of different occupations that end with *-er*. Discuss what each person does and how it relates to the base word, such as *baker* and *bake*.

© Scott Foresman 2

climb	comb	lamb	kneel	knit	knot

Pick a word from the box to match each clue.
Write the word on the line.

1. You do this to a hill. _____

2. It rhymes with *heel.* _____

Change one letter in each word to make a word from the box.
Write the new word on the line.

3. come

   _____

4. lame

   _____

5. know

   _____

6. knot

   _____

Pick a word from the box to finish each sentence.
Write the word on the line.

story	able

7. I know a great _____ .

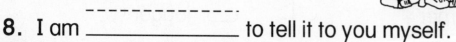

8. I am _____ to tell it to you myself.

Notes for Home: Your child spelled words with *mb* and *kn* where one letter in each pair is silent *(climb, knot)*, as well as two frequently used words: *story, able.* **Home Activity:** Using these spelling words, work with your child to write a story about a little lamb.

© Scott Foresman 2

Family Times

Yawning Dawn

Missing: One Stuffed Rabbit

My Dog's Paw

We saw a sign at our local vet.
"Please take me home. I'll be your pet!"
This little dog sat on bits of straw.
We saw that he had hurt his paw.
We brought him home but he couldn't crawl.
We wrapped his paw in our mother's shawl.
When we unwrapped his little paw,
He used his paw to scratch his jaw.
Now who can jump up?
Now who can crawl?
Our little dog will come when we call.

This rhyme includes words your child is working with in school: words spelled with *aw* and *ough* (*paw, brought*) and words with *gn, wh,* and *wr,* where one consonant in each letter pair is silent (*sign, who, wrapped*). Sing "My Dog's Paw" with your child. As you sing, shout the words with *aw* and *ough*.

(fold here)

Name: _____

You are your child's first and best teacher!

Here are ways to help your child practice skills while having fun!

Day 1 Your child is learning to read words with *aw* and *ough* that have the same vowel sound (*saw, thought*). When reading together, look for words with *aw* and *ough* that have this vowel sound, such as *draw, straw, bought, brought.*

Day 2 Your child is learning to read these words: *family, finally, morning, paper,* and *really.* Challenge your child to write a sentence using as many of these words as possible.

Day 3 Read a story with your child. As you read, point out the characters' actions. Ask your child to make judgments by asking questions such as: *Why do you think that character did that? Is that a good way to act?*

Day 4 Give your child verbal instructions to follow such as: *Hop on your left foot. Wave your right hand. Pick up the blue button.*

Day 5 Work with your child to write instructions that explain how to play a favorite game.

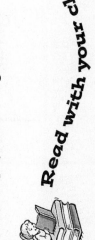

Read with your child EVERY DAY!

© Scott Foresman 2

Silent-Letter Spins

Materials paper circle, paper clip, pencil, 1 button per player

Game Directions

1. Make a simple spinner as shown and take turns spinning a letter pair.

2. Toss a button on the gameboard to try to land on a word that has the same letter pair. If a player fails to land on a word with the same letter pair, the player loses his or her turn.

3. If a player lands on a word that has the same letter pair, says the word correctly, and identifies its silent consonant, he or she earns 1 point.

4. The first player to earn 5 points wins!

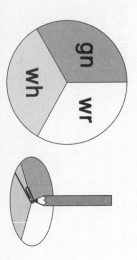

sign	who	wreck
write	design	whole
who's	wreath	gnaw
gnarled	whose	wrong
who'll	gnat	wrapping

Name _____

Circle a word to finish each sentence.
Write the word on the line.

He b**ough**t a dr**aw**ing.

_____

loan   lawn

- - - - - - - - - - - - - - - - - - -

1. I looked at the _____ .

saw   swamp

- - - - - - - - - - - - - - - - - - -

2. What do you think I _____ ?

toad   thought

- - - - - - - - - - - - - - - - - - -

3. I _____ it was a dragon.

claws   climbs

- - - - - - - - - - - - - - - - - - -

4. It had nasty _____ .

jays   jaws

- - - - - - - - - - - - - - - - - - -

5. It was Tom inside the _____ !

Notes for Home: Your child read words with *aw* and *ough* (drawing, bought). **Home Activity:** Ask your child to make up a story about an animal. Challenge your child to use words with this vowel sound and these spellings.

© Scott Foresman 2

Circle a word to finish each sentence.
Write the word on the line.

wrench

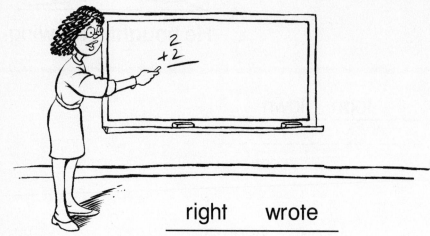

right   wrote
_____
- - - - - - - - - - - - -

1. The teacher _____ the problem.

hill   whole
_____
- - - - - - - - - - - - -

2. The _____ class watched her.

sign   swan
_____
- - - - - - - - - - - - -

3. She drew a plus _____ .

how   who
_____
- - - - - - - - - - - - -

4. She asked _____ knew the answer.

wrong   rode
_____
- - - - - - - - - - - - -

5. I was happy my answer wasn't _____ .

Notes for Home: Your child read words with the letters pairs *gn, wh,* and *wr* in which one consonant is silent, as in *sign, whole,* and *write.* **Home Activity:** Ask your child to make a sign for a new household product using words with these letter pairs.

© Scott Foresman 2

Pick a word from the box to finish each sentence.
Write the word on the line.

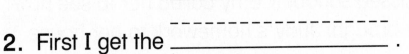

| family | finally | morning | paper | really |

1. I get up early every _____ .

2. First I get the _____ .

3. Next, my _____ cooks.

4. _____ , we eat.

5. I _____ like mornings!

Notes for Home: This week your child is learning to read the words *family, finally, morning, paper,* and *really.* **Home Activity:** Ask your child to make the front page of a newspaper and write a story about a family activity. Encourage your child to use the listed words.

© Scott Foresman 2

Name _____

Read the story.
Answer the questions.

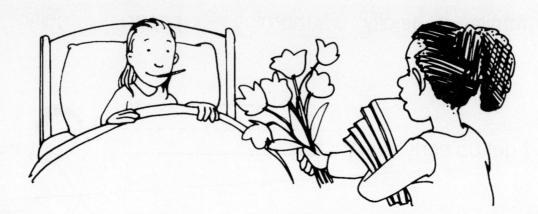

Judy was sick and missed school. Cathy called her to see how she was feeling. She brought Judy's homework to her house.

_____

1. Is Cathy a good friend? _____

2. Why do you think so?

_____

_____

3. **Think** about something nice you did for a friend.
   Write a sentence that tells what you did.

_____

_____

_____

_____

Notes for Home: Your child made a judgment about a character in a story.
Home Activity: Read a story with your child. Ask questions about why your child thinks someone did something, and if your child thinks it was a good idea.

70 **Making Judgments**

Level 2.2

© Scott Foresman 2

Adverbs can tell how, when, or where something happens.
Quickly is an **adverb**.

Jane runs **quickly**.

Circle the adverb in each sentence.
Write the adverb on the line.

1. Our Thanksgiving play is today.

_____
_____

2. We came to school early.

_____
_____

3. We practice inside.

_____
_____

4. We sing loudly.

_____
_____

5. We walk softly.

_____
_____

Notes for Home: Your child identified adverbs—words that tell how, when, or where something happens. *Home Activity:* Give your child simple commands that use adverbs to tell how to do the action. *(Clap your hands softly.)*

© Scott Foresman 2

Name _____

Pick a word from the box to match each clue.
Write the word on the line.

calm	family	finally	gathered
hospital	morning	paper	really

1. a place where sick or hurt people go

   _____

   _____

2. something to write on

   _____

   _____

3. mother, father, brothers, and sisters

   _____

   _____

4. came together

   _____

   _____

5. quiet

   _____

   _____

6. at last

   _____

   _____

7. beginning of the day

   _____

   _____

8. very much, truly

   _____

   _____

Notes for Home: Your child used word clues to practice new vocabulary words.
Home Activity: Make a simple crossword puzzle with your child using some of these vocabulary words. Use the clues above or write your own clues.

© Scott Foresman 2

w<u>a</u>ter

w<u>al</u>king

s<u>au</u>ce

Pick the word in ( ) that has the same vowel sound as **sauce**.
Circle the word to finish each sentence.

1. The water comes out of the (glass / faucet).

2. Our teacher (calls / says) hello to us.

3. I like (butter / salt) on my food.

4. I hurt my knee (because / when) I fell down.

5. He hit the (bell / ball) hard.

6. I like to draw with (markers / chalk).

7. This shirt is too (large / small).

8. We were late, and it was all my (fault / mistake).

Find the word that has the same vowel sound as the picture.
Mark the space to show your answer.

9. ⊂⊃ told
   ⊂⊃ talk
   ⊂⊃ take

10. ⊂⊃ ant
    ⊂⊃ able
    ⊂⊃ author

Notes for Home: Your child reviewed words that have the vowel sound heard in *sauce* spelled *a, al,* and *au.* **Home Activity:** Write some of the words with this vowel sound listed above. Have your child create new words with this vowel sound by changing a few letters in each word.

© Scott Foresman 2

awful   bought   claw   draw   saw   straw

Write four words from the box that rhyme with **jaw**.

1. _____

2. _____

3. _____

4. _____

Pick a word from the box that has nearly the same meaning as the word or words below.
Write the word on the line.

5. bad

_____

6. sketch

_____

7. paid for

_____

8. looked

_____

Add -ly to each word below to make a word from the box.
Write the new word on the line.

really   finally

9. final _____

10. real _____

Notes for Home: Your child spelled words with the vowel sound in *ball* spelled *aw* and *ough* and two frequently used words: *really, finally.* **Home Activity:** Say each spelling word, and then use it in a sentence. Repeat the word, and have your child write it.

© Scott Foresman 2

Name _____

Write steps in the right order.

Go to the store.
Buy peanut butter, jelly, and bread.

Read the steps.
Write 1, 2, 3, 4 to show the right order.

_____

_____ 1. Add jelly on top of the peanut butter.

_____ 2. Set out two slices of toast.

_____ 3. Put the other slice of toast on top of the jelly.

_____ 4. Put peanut butter on one slice.

Write a title that tells what these steps are about.

5. _____

_____

© Scott Foresman 2

Notes for Home: Your child put steps in a process in order. *Home Activity:* Prepare dinner or a treat with your child. As you prepare your food, discuss the order in which things need to be done. Later ask your child to retell you the steps you took in the order you did them.

Circle the adverb in each sentence.

1. We go to music class weekly.

2. We will see the music teacher soon.

3. I walk into the classroom quickly.

4. Peter arrives last.

5. The teacher wants us all to sing loudly.

6. We join our voices cheerfully.

7. We go to recess outside.

8. We play games happily.

Pick two of the adverbs circled above.
Write a new sentence using each adverb.

9. _____

10. _____

Notes for Home: Your child identified and wrote adverbs—words that tell how, when, or where something happens. *Home Activity:* Give your child short sentences and ask him or her to add adverbs to them. Discuss how adverbs can make sentences more interesting.

© Scott Foresman 2

Part 1: Vocabulary

Find the word that best fits in each sentence.
Mark the space for your answer.

1. We went to see Grandpa in the _____ .
   - ⬭ team
   - ⬭ hospital
   - ⬭ family

2. The sun comes up in the _____ .
   - ⬭ paper
   - ⬭ head
   - ⬭ morning

3. Mom told me to _____ down.
   - ⬭ clean
   - ⬭ calm
   - ⬭ fix

4. Sam _____ all his toys together.
   - ⬭ giggled
   - ⬭ gathered
   - ⬭ exclaimed

5. His shirt is _____ yellow.
   - ⬭ another
   - ⬭ finally
   - ⬭ really

© Scott Foresman · 2

GO ON ➡

Part 2: Comprehension

Read each question.
Mark the space for your answer.

6. Why are the children excited on Friday?
   - ⬭ There is no school the next day.
   - ⬭ They are all going on a trip.
   - ⬭ Someone will take Coco home.

7. Coco goes everywhere with his —
   - ⬭ diary.
   - ⬭ rabbit.
   - ⬭ bowl.

8. How did Janine feel when Coco got lost?
   - ⬭ friendly
   - ⬭ sad
   - ⬭ excited

9. Janine guessed where Coco was from the —
   - ⬭ Lost and Found Department.
   - ⬭ frog at the hospital.
   - ⬭ "Toy Drive" sign.

10. Was Janine right to let Teresa keep Coco?
    - ⬭ Yes, because Coco made Teresa feel better.
    - ⬭ No, because Coco belongs to Mrs. Robin.
    - ⬭ Yes, because Coco will get lost again.

STOP

© Scott Foresman 2

Name _____

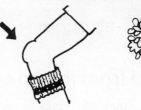 

Circle the word for each picture. <u>kn</u>ee   li<u>mb</u>

1. 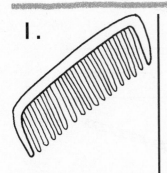	2. 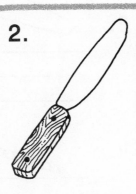	3.	4. 
comb cub	nice knife	lamb lab	nut knot
5. 	6. 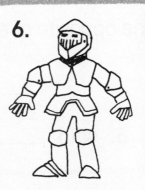	7. 	8. 
club climb	kite knight	thumb thump	kitten knit

Find the word that has a silent consonant.
Mark the space to show your answer.

9. ⬭ know
   ⬭ kind
   ⬭ kiss

10. ⬭ plums
    ⬭ plumber
    ⬭ plank

Notes for Home: Your child reviewed words with *kn* and *mb* where one letter in each pair is silent as in <u>kn</u>ee and li<u>mb</u>. **Home Activity:** Make picture cards of words with *kn* and *mb* with your child. Take turns picking cards and writing a sentence about each word pictured.

© Scott Foresman 2

Name _____

awful   bought   claw   draw   saw   straw

Pick a word from the box to match each picture.
Write the word on the line.

1.

_____
- - - - - - - - - - - - - - - -
_____

2.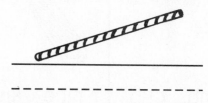

_____
- - - - - - - - - - - - - - - -
_____

3.

_____
- - - - - - - - - - - - - - - -
_____

4.

_____
- - - - - - - - - - - - - - - -
_____

Pick a word from the box that is the opposite of each word below.
Write the word on the line.

5. great _____

6. sold _____

Pick a word from the box to match each clue.
Write the word on the line.

really   finally

7. at last

_____
- - - - - - - - - - - - -
_____

8. I felt _____ sad.

_____
- - - - - - - - - - - - -
_____

 Notes for Home: Your child spelled words with *aw* and *ough* that have the vowel sound heard in *straw* and *bought*. **Home Activity:** Hold a spelling bee. Give your child a word, have him or her repeat the word, and then spell it aloud.

© Scott Foresman 2

One word in each sentence is **not** correct.
Circle the incorrect word.
Write the word correctly on the line.
Hint: Use words that end in **-er** to compare two things.
Use words that end in **-est** to compare more than two.

1. Use a ball big than a softball. _____

2. The higher score you can get is ten. _____

3. Use your fast player to run. _____

4. Sara is the taller player on our team. _____

5. Mike is a hardest kicker than Tom. _____

 Notes for Home: Your child corrected comparative adjectives that end in *-er* and superlative adjectives that end in *-est*. **Home Activity:** Look through a picture book with your child. Have him or her make comparisons about the characters using adjectives that end in *-er* or *-est*.

© Scott Foresman 2

Words I Can Now Read and Write

_____   _____
- - - - - - - - - - - - - - - - - -   - - - - - - - - - - - - - - - - - -
_____   _____
- - - - - - - - - - - - - - - - - -   - - - - - - - - - - - - - - - - - -
_____   _____
- - - - - - - - - - - - - - - - - -   - - - - - - - - - - - - - - - - - -
_____   _____
- - - - - - - - - - - - - - - - - -   - - - - - - - - - - - - - - - - - -
_____   _____
- - - - - - - - - - - - - - - - - -   - - - - - - - - - - - - - - - - - -
_____   _____
- - - - - - - - - - - - - - - - - -
                                        _____
                                        - - - - - - - - - - - - - - - - - -
                                        _____
                                        - - - - - - - - - - - - - - - - - -
                                        _____
                                        - - - - - - - - - - - - - - - - - -
                                        _____

© Scott Foresman 2

Family Times

Space Dreams

Man on the Moon

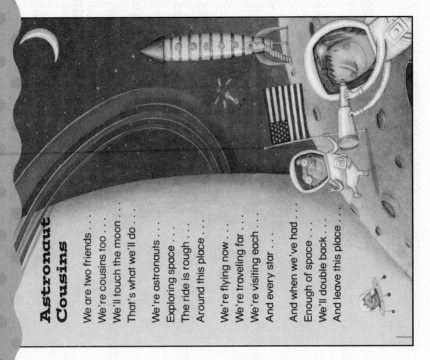

Astronaut Cousins

We are two friends . . .
We're cousins too . . .
We'll touch the moon . . . .
That's what we'll do . . . .

We're astronauts . . . .
Exploring space . . . .
The ride is rough . . . .
Around this place . . . .

We're flying now . . . .
We're traveling far . . .
We're visiting each . . . .
And every star . . . .

And when we've had . . . .
Enough of space . . . .
We'll double back . . . .
And leave this place . . . .

This rhyme includes words your child is working with in school: words with short *u* spelled *ou* (*cousins*) and words with more than one syllable (*astronauts*). Sing "Cousins in Space" with your child. For each word with more than one syllable, clap out each syllable together.

(fold here)

Name: _____

© Scott Foresman 2

You are your child's first and best teacher!

Here are ways to help your child practice skills while having fun!

Day 1 Write the following words on slips of paper: *could, count, country, couple, cousin, double, down, dot, through, thought, trouble, truck, you, young.* Have your child identify the words with the short *u* vowel sound heard in *cup*.

Day 2 Have your child write a list of questions to ask an astronaut, using these words: *began, Earth, ever, remember, try.*

Day 3 Read a paragraph from a book or a newspaper together. Have your child explain the most important idea of the paragraph.

Day 4 Challenge your child to summarize the important events of a story or TV show in a few sentences.

Day 5 Read a story or magazine article with your child. Have him or her point out the pronouns *he, she, it, we, they, you* and identify who or what each pronoun represents.

Read with your child EVERY DAY!

Animal Match

Materials index cards, markers, bag

Game Directions

1. Use index cards to make a set of picture cards with matching word cards as shown.

2. Place the picture cards face down on the table. Place the word cards in a bag.

3. Take turns drawing a word card and flipping over a picture card to try to make a match.

4. Players keep each pair made. If cards don't match, the player turns over the picture card and returns the word card to the bag.

5. When all matches have been made, the player with the most pairs wins!

bulldog

chipmunk

crocodile

kangaroo

lizard

octopus

porcupine

walrus

Pick the word with the **short u** sound you hear in **double**.
Circle the word to finish each sentence.

1. We spent a night in the _____ .

outdoors
country
house

2. My _____ and I saw many stars.

aunt
cousin
hound

3. They seemed close enough to _____ .

count
touch
bounce

4. A _____ of stars were very bright.

couple
group
outline

5. One group of stars looks like a _____ bear.

cute
young
proud

Notes for Home: Your child read words in which the short *u* sound is spelled *ou* as in *double*.
Home Activity: Find words with *ou* as you read together. Have your child say each word aloud
and tell whether it has the same vowel sound as *double*.

© Scott Foresman 2

Name _____

Circle the word for each picture.

1. 	2. 	3. 	4. 
rocket record	pilot plot	battle basket	plant planet
5. 	6. 	7.	8.
circle circus	hammer hamper	little lizard	button butter

Draw a picture for each word.

9. astronaut

10. elephant

Notes for Home: Your child identified words with two or more syllables by sounding out more familiar word parts, such as *rock • et* for *rocket.* **Home Activity:** As you read with your child, point out words with more than one syllable. Help your child read each word.

© Scott Foresman 2

Pick a word from the box to finish each sentence.
Write the word on the line.

| began | Earth | ever | remember | try |

_____

1. Nina _____ to build a rocket.

_____

2. I will _____ to fly.

_____

3. _____ to wear a seat belt.

_____

4. Will you _____ come back?

_____

5. I'll come back to _____ soon!

Notes for Home: This week your child is learning to read the words *began, Earth, ever, remember,* and *try*. **Home Activity:** Have your child pretend that he or she is on the moon. Have your child use these words to write a letter home.

© Scott Foresman 2

Read the paragraph.
Write a word or two that tells the topic.
Write a sentence that tells the main idea.
Draw a picture of the main idea.

A United States astronaut was the first person to set foot on the moon. His name was Neil Armstrong. It happened on July 20, 1969. The name of the spaceship was the *Apollo 11*. The world watched on TV as he walked on the moon's surface.

_____

1. Topic: _____

_____

2. Main Idea: _____

_____

_____

_____

3.

Notes for Home: Your child has been learning to identify the main idea of a paragraph.
Home Activity: Read aloud a paragraph from a nonfiction article with your child. Then have your child tell you the main idea of the paragraph.

© Scott Foresman 2

Level 2.2

A **pronoun** is a word that takes the place of a noun or nouns.
The astronaut went to the moon.
He went to the moon.
The rocket landed.
It landed.

Pick a pronoun from the box to take the place of the underlined word or words.
Write the pronoun on the line.

| he | she | it | we | they |

_____ 1. <u>Eric and his sister</u> came to visit.

_____ 2. <u>My friends and I</u> watched a TV program.

_____ 3. <u>The program</u> was about the first moon walk.

_____ 4. <u>Lisa</u> wants to be an astronaut.

_____ 5. <u>Eric</u> would rather stay on Earth!

Notes for Home: Your child used pronouns to take the place of nouns in sentences. ***Home Activity:*** Find a newspaper or magazine article that your child can read. Underline some of the nouns and have your child replace them with pronouns.

© Scott Foresman 2

Name _____

Pick a word from the box to finish the sentence.
Write the word on the line.

began	circled	Earth	ever	remember	rockets	try

_____

1. Did I _____ tell you about my space trip?

2. Tell me again. I don't _____ it all.

3. My rocket _____ Earth three times.

4. I _____ to get a little scared.

5. I was glad to get back to _____ !

6. I never wanted to _____ flying again!

7. Now I watch _____ launch only on TV.

Notes for Home: Your child used vocabulary words to complete sentences. *Home Activity:*
Encourage your child to use some of the vocabulary words to write a description of a trip
to space.

© Scott Foresman 2

Name _____

Put each group of words in **ABC order**.
Pick a word in ( ) that comes between the two words shown.
Write the word on the line.

(the / toy)

1. tip _____ try

(clap / cent)

2. chill _____ come

(bib / bug)

3. beg _____ black

(wring / why)

4. wet _____ will

(and / air)

5. age _____ all

(got / give)

6. glow _____ grow

(dog / duty)

7. dizzy _____ dry

(sky / snow)

8. sick _____ smile

(ever / eye)

9. erase _____ extra

(brag / bed)

10. bad _____ boy

Notes for Home: Your child alphabetized words by looking at the second letter in words that begin with the same letter. This skill will help your child better use a glossary or dictionary.
Home Activity: Help your child use the telephone book to look up the names of people you know.

© Scott Foresman 2

str<u>aw</u>   b<u>ough</u>t

Circle the word for each picture.

1. 	2. 	3. 	4. 
say saw	lane lawn	shawl shell	thought thorn

5. 	6. 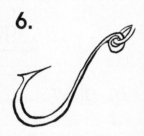	7. 	8. 
cuff cough	hook hawk	fought foot	dawn down

Find the word that has the same vowel sound as the picture.
Mark the space to show your answer.

9. ⬭ low
   ⬭ law
   ⬭ laugh

10. ⬭ old
    ⬭ ought
    ⬭ own

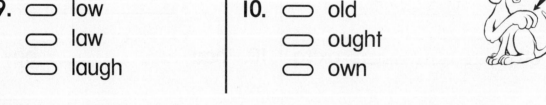

 Notes for Home: Your child reviewed words spelled with *aw* or *ough* that have the vowel sound heard in *straw* and *bought*. **Home Activity:** Help your child write sentences using words with *aw* and *ough* listed above. Then have your child read the sentences aloud.

92   Phonics: /ò/ Vowel Patterns *aw, ough* Review

Level 2.2

© Scott Foresman 2

camera   carry   follow   lesson   pretty   suddenly

Write four words from the box that have two syllables.

1. _____

2. _____

3. _____

4. _____

Write two words from the box that have three syllables.

5. _____

6. _____

Pick a word from the box that is the opposite of each word below.
Write the word on the line.

7. ugly _____

8. drop _____

Say the word for each picture.
Write the word from the box that has
the same beginning sound.

ever   began

9.

_____

10.

_____

Notes for Home: Your child spelled words that have more than one syllable, such as *suddenly,* and two frequently used words: *ever, began.* **Home Activity:** Help your child use these spelling words to write sentences. Have your child read each sentence aloud.

© Scott Foresman 2

Name _____

Circle the word or words in the first sentence that the underlined pronoun replaces.

1. We are watching the news. <u>It</u> shows a moon landing.

2. Jack and I just sat down. <u>We</u> haven't watched long.

3. Where are the three pigs? Are <u>they</u> coming?

4. That astronaut is brave. <u>He</u> is very far from home.

5. Bessie doesn't care. <u>She</u> jumped over the moon long ago.

Pick a pronoun from the box to replace each group of words.
Write the pronoun on the line.

| he | it | she | they | we |

6. you and I
_____

7. the rocket
_____

8. my mom
_____

9. Paul and his dog
_____

10. Jennie's dad _____

Notes for Home: Your child identified words that the pronouns *he, she, it, we,* and *they* replace. **Home Activity:** As you read a book with your child, pause and ask your child to change some of the nouns to pronouns.

© Scott Foresman 2

Part 1: Vocabulary

Find the word that best fits in each sentence.
Mark the space for your answer.

1. Have you _____ looked at the moon?
   - ⬭ able
   - ⬭ ever
   - ⬭ done

2. Lee will _____ to come to the game.
   - ⬭ guess
   - ⬭ use
   - ⬭ try

3. The sun _____ to shine.
   - ⬭ began
   - ⬭ gathered
   - ⬭ circled

4. Three _____ fly into the sky.
   - ⬭ paws
   - ⬭ dinosaurs
   - ⬭ rockets

5. I can't _____ the cat's name.
   - ⬭ remember
   - ⬭ Earth
   - ⬭ try

© Scott Foresman 2

GO ON ➡

Part 2: Comprehension

Read each question.
Mark the space for your answer.

6. Before 1969, no one had ever —
   - ⬭ gone into space.
   - ⬭ walked on the moon.
   - ⬭ made rockets fly.

7. What happened first?
   - ⬭ *Saturn 5* took off.
   - ⬭ Armstrong took pictures on the moon.
   - ⬭ The *Eagle* landed.

8. Collins did not walk on the moon because —
   - ⬭ he was sick.
   - ⬭ he had to fly *Columbia*.
   - ⬭ he did not want to.

9. The writer wanted mostly to tell about —
   - ⬭ the first walk on the moon.
   - ⬭ how to fly rockets.
   - ⬭ what we see on TV.

10. How do you know that men walked on the moon?
    - ⬭ The moon remembers the men.
    - ⬭ They came down in the Pacific Ocean.
    - ⬭ They brought moon rocks back to Earth.

STOP

© Scott Foresman 2

Name _____

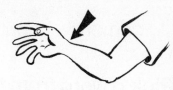

<u>gn</u>ats

<u>Wh</u>o's there?

<u>wr</u>ist

Circle the word for each picture.

1. 	2. 	3. 	4. 
whole will	wrench when	wrapped want	write white

5. 	6. 	7.	8.
sign sing	design desk	gown gnaw	breath wreath

Find the word that has the silent consonant.
Mark the space to show your answer.

9. ⬭ wind
   ⬭ who
   ⬭ wood

10. ⬭ wreck
    ⬭ wet
    ⬭ wig

Notes for Home: Your child reviewed words spelled with *gn, wh,* and *wr.* ***Home Activity:***
Write some of the following words on index cards and help your child practice reading them:
gnash, gnat, gnaw, gnome, sign, design, whole, who, whose, wholly, wrap, wreath, wrong.

© Scott Foresman 2

| camera | carry | follow | lesson | pretty | suddenly |

Pick a word from the box to match each clue.
Write the word on the line.

1. not lead

_____

2. hold

_____

3. something you learn

_____

4. lovely

_____

5. It takes pictures.

_____

6. quickly

_____

Pick a word from the box to match each clue.
Write the word on the line.

| ever | began |

7. It rhymes with *never*. _____

8. It means the same as "started." _____

Notes for Home: Your child spelled words with more than one syllable, such as *suddenly,* and two frequently used words: *ever, began.* **Home Activity:** Have your child write sentences using these spelling words and read each sentence aloud, clapping hands for each syllable.

© Scott Foresman 2

Family Times

Two Lunches at the Mill

Going to Town

All Across the Country

Long ago we chopped down trees.
Built our houses, one, two, three.
Life was simple all around me.
All across the country.

People in the kitchen, do, re, mi.
Cakes on the table, one, two, three.
Sit on the benches, sit with me.
All across the country.

Round up the horses, ride with me.
Pick up the boxes, one, two, three.
Gather up your dresses, dance with me.
All across the country.

This rhyme includes words your child is working with in school: plural words where adding -s or -es adds a syllable *(houses)* and words with the schwa vowel sound spelled *a* and *le (across, people)*. Read the rhyme with your child and act it out.

(fold here)

Name: _____

© Scott Foresman 2

You *are* your child's first and best teacher!

Here are ways to help your child practice skills while having fun!

Day 1 Ask your child to circle all the words in a newspaper article that end in *le* such as *people.* Help your child read the circled words aloud and listen for the sound *le* represents.

Day 2 Have your child use the words *behind, only, sure, upon,* and *word* to write about a family trip.

Day 3 Encourage your child to draw a character from a favorite story. Help your child write a caption that describes what the character is like.

Day 4 Your child is learning how to give demonstrations. Encourage your child to demonstrate how to make a sandwich or other simple food items, explaining each step aloud in order.

Day 5 Help your child write a series of short steps that explain how to operate a simple household appliance, such as a toaster. Post the information beside the appliance.

Read with your child EVERY DAY!

Three Across

Materials   25 colored paper squares per player (one color per player)

Game Directions

1. Players take turns placing a colored square on a word in a tic tac toe square.

2. To keep the colored square in place, the player must correctly write and say the plural of that word.

3. The first player to line up three squares down, across, or diagonally wins!

cage	house	stage	change	hose
age	wage	dish	race	lunch
fence	beach	piece	prize	place
orange	price	nose	fox	rose
glass	page	nurse	horse	size

Name _____

Amanda likes only things that have the **schwa sound** in their names. She doesn't like things that don't have this sound in their names.

b<u>a</u>lloon

Circle a word to show what Amanda likes.
Write the word on the line.

apples   berries

1. She likes _____ .

pickles   cabbage

2. She likes _____ .

yellow   purple

3. She likes _____ .

bananas   raisins

4. She likes _____ .

beyond   across

5. She likes to walk _____ the park.

Notes for Home: Your child identified words with the schwa sound which can be spelled with *a* or *le* (b<u>a</u>lloon and *peop<u>le</u>*). **Home Activity:** Have your child read aloud words that end in *le* in which *le* represents the same vowel sound as in *people*.

© Scott Foresman 2

Level 2.2

Phonics: Schwa Sound in *across* and *people* **101**

Add -s or **-es** to the noun in ( ) to show more than one.
Write the new noun on the line to finish each sentence.

(house)

_____

- - - - - - - - - - - - - - - -

1. The _____ were on the hill.

(bush)

_____

- - - - - - - - - - - - - - - -

2. Their yards were full of _____ .

(fence)

_____

- - - - - - - - - - - - - - - -

3. Flowers grew along the _____.

(place)

_____

- - - - - - - - - - - - - - - -

4. In some _____ , there were big trees.

(horse)

_____

- - - - - - - - - - - - - - - -

5. The _____ pulled a wagon.

Notes for Home: Your child added *-s* and *-es* to nouns to make them plural. *Home Activity:*
Have your child make these words plural: *face, cage, vase, size.* Point out that adding *-s* to
words that end in *e* adds a syllable *(face, faces).*

© Scott Foresman 2

Pick a word from the box to finish each sentence.
Write the word on the line.

| behind | only | sure | upon | word |

1. Young Will sat _____ the wagon seat.

2. He was so happy that he could not say a _____ .

3. He had been to town _____ one time before.

4. Pa was not _____ how long they would stay.

5. They had left their cabin far _____ them.

Notes for Home: This week your child is learning to read the words *behind, only, sure, upon,* and *word.* **Home Activity:** Challenge your child to use some of these words to write about some family photographs.

© Scott Foresman 2

High-Frequency Words **103**

Name _____

Look at each picture to see what it shows about the person.
Pick a word from the box that tells what each person is like.
Write the word on the line.

fair	funny	greedy	mean
nice	shy	smart	sneaky

1. Amy gets good grades _____

   _ _ _ _ _ _ _ _ _ _ _ _ _
   because she is _____ .

2.
   _____

   _ _ _ _ _ _ _ _ _ _ _ _ _
   Jack is a _____ friend.

3. We let Matt judge the game _____

   _ _ _ _ _ _ _ _ _ _ _ _
   because he is _____ .

4.
   _____

   _ _ _ _ _ _ _ _ _ _ _ _
   Sally is very _____ .

5. Billy does not always raise his hand _____

   _ _ _ _ _ _ _ _ _ _ _ _ _
   because he can be _____ .

Notes for Home: Your child used word and picture clues to figure out what someone is like.
Home Activity: When you read with your child, pause to ask her or him what a certain character is like. Then ask why your child thinks so.

© Scott Foresman 2

Level 2.2

He, **she**, and **it** are **pronouns**
that name only one.
He is eight years old.
We and **they** are **pronouns**
that name more than one.
They are friends.

Pick a pronoun from the box to take the place of the
underlined word or words.
Write the pronoun on the line.

| he | she | it | we | they |

_____
_____ 1. Mary's family moved west in a big wagon.

_____ 2. The wagon top was like a round tent.

_____ 3. Mary's father drove the wagon all day.

_____ 4. Will my family and I ever get there?

_____ 5. Mary helped her mother fix meals.

Notes for Home: Your child used singular and plural pronouns to replace subjects in
sentences. **Home Activity:** Ask your child questions about what his or her class did that day.
Encourage your child to answer using the pronouns *he, she, it, we,* and *they.*

© Scott Foresman 2

Pick a word from the box to finish each sentence.
Write the word on the line.

behind	crops	edge	sure	trade	upon	word

1. Annie's family came to _____ at the store.

2. They sold some of the _____ they grew.

3. Mr. Clay stood _____ the store counter.

4. Annie was not _____ what to buy.

5. A ribbon hung over the _____ of the counter.

6. A jar of candy sat _____ the counter.

7. She pointed to the jar without saying a _____ .

Notes for Home: Your child used new vocabulary words to complete sentences. *Home Activity:* Use these words to pretend you and your child are living out west a century ago.

© Scott Foresman 2

Name _____

Read each clue.
Look at each picture.
Write the letters to finish each word.
Hint: They all have the same vowel sound as **double**.

d<u>ou</u>ble scoop

---

1. relatives

_____
c _____ sins

2. not smooth

_____
r _____ gh

---

3. not old

_____
y _____ ng

4. not a good thing

_____
tr _____ ble

---

5. not a city

_____
c _____ ntry

6. not easy

_____
t _____ gh

Find the word that has the same vowel sound as **double**.
Mark the space to show your answer.

7. ⬭ couple
   ⬭ cute
   ⬭ cows

8. ⬭ tool
   ⬭ touch
   ⬭ tube

 Notes for Home: Your child reviewed words in which the short *u* sound is spelled *ou,* as in *dou̲ble*. **Home Activity:** Write short sentences using some of the words with *ou* above: *country, couple, rough, tough, trouble, young.* Ask your child to read them aloud.

© Scott Foresman 2

Name _____

| blouse | blouses | place | places | race | races |

Read the head at the top of each column.
Write the words from the box that belong in each column.

Names One	**Names More Than One**
1. _____	2. _____
3. _____	4. _____
5. _____	6. _____

Pick a word from the box to match each picture.
Write the word on the line.

7.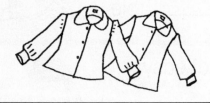

8.

_____

_____

Pick a word from the box to match each clue.
Write the word on the line.

| only | word |

9. a group of letters _____

10. rhymes with *lonely* _____

Notes for Home: Your child spelled pairs of singular and plural words and two frequently
used words: *only, word*. **Home Activity:** Help your child use these words to write newspaper
ads and announcements.

© Scott Foresman 2

Name _____

Circle a pronoun to take the place of the underlined words.

1. The children are playing ball.
   He   We   They

2. Tom throws the ball.
   He   We   They

3. Susan catches the ball from Tom.
   He   It   She

4. "Mary and I want the ball!"
   He   We   Her

5. The ball will be thrown to Mary and Nan.
   It   He   They
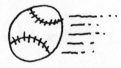

Circle the pronouns that name one.
Underline the pronouns that name more than one.

6.–10. he we they she it

Notes for Home: Your child reviewed using pronouns that name only one person, place, or thing and pronouns that name more than one. **Home Activity:** Find a picture that shows activity. Have your child use pronouns to describe what is happening goin the picture.

© Scott Foresman 2

Test-Taking Tips

1. Write your name on the test.

2. Read each question twice.

3. Read all the answer choices for the question.

4. Mark your answer carefully.

5. Check your answer.

© Scott Foresman 2

Part 1: Vocabulary

Find the word that best fits in each sentence.
Mark the space for your answer.

1. Are you _____ we can go in?
   - ⊂⊃ able
   - ⊂⊃ sure
   - ⊂⊃ upon

2. What does that _____ mean?
   - ⊂⊃ edge
   - ⊂⊃ city
   - ⊂⊃ word

3. Jay and I sat _____ Mom and Dad.
   - ⊂⊃ across
   - ⊂⊃ until
   - ⊂⊃ behind

4. The farmer planted his _____ .
   - ⊂⊃ crops
   - ⊂⊃ feathers
   - ⊂⊃ paws

5. Meg wanted to _____ a book for my doll.
   - ⊂⊃ trade
   - ⊂⊃ peel
   - ⊂⊃ follow

GO ON ➡

© Scott Foresman 2

Part 2: Comprehension

Read each question.
Mark the space for your answer.

6. Laura lived in a little house in the —
   - ⬭ woods.
   - ⬭ town of Pepin.
   - ⬭ city.

7. Pa said they would all go to town as soon as he —
   - ⬭ got cleaned up.
   - ⬭ had enough tools.
   - ⬭ planted the crops.

8. How did Laura and Mary feel about going to town?
   - ⬭ sad
   - ⬭ excited
   - ⬭ terrible

9. What is another good name for this story?
   - ⬭ "A Day by the Lake"
   - ⬭ "The Red Dress"
   - ⬭ "A Special Day"

10. When Laura first saw the town, she was surprised because —
    - ⬭ there were so many houses.
    - ⬭ the town was so small.
    - ⬭ there were no people.

STOP

© Scott Foresman 2

Name _____

Circle the word for each picture.

 le**tt**er

---

1.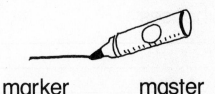

marker master

2.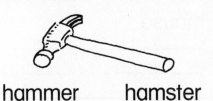

hammer hamster

3.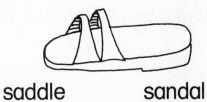

saddle sandal

4.

surfing surprise

5.

singers sisters

6.

thirsty thirty

7.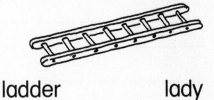

ladder lady

8.

candle camel

Find the word that has the same middle consonant sound as the picture.

Mark the space to show your answer.

9. ◯ carrot
  ◯ kitten
  ◯ muffin

10. ◯ dragon
   ◯ tuba
   ◯ buttons

 Notes for Home: Your child reviewed words that have more than one syllable. ***Home Activity:*** Help your child read ads in newspapers. Sound out each syllable. Circle words that have more than one syllable.

© Scott Foresman 2

| blouse | blouses | place | places | race | races |

Write a word from the box that rhymes with each word below.

1. mouse

   _____

   - - - - - - - - - - - - - - - -

   _____

2. houses

   _____

   - - - - - - - - - - - - - - - -

   _____

Change one letter in each word to make a word from the box.
Write the new word on the line.

3. faces

   _____

   - - - - - - - - - - - - - - - -

   _____

4. rice

   _____

   - - - - - - - - - - - - - - - -

   _____

5. plates

   _____

   - - - - - - - - - - - - - - - -

   _____

6. plane

   _____

   - - - - - - - - - - - - - - - -

   _____

Unscramble the letters to make a word from the box.
Write the word on the line.

| only | word |

7. odwr

   _____

   - - - - - - - - - - - - - - - -

8. lyon

   _____

   - - - - - - - - - - - - - - - -

Notes for Home: Your child spelled pairs of singular and plural words, and two frequently used words: *only, word*. **Home Activity:** Write a spelling word. Ask your child to use the letters to make as many words as possible *(blouses = blouse, blue, bus, be, us, less).*

© Scott Foresman 2

Family Times

A True Boating Family   **Riding the Ferry with Captain Cruz**

Peggy Sue

My name is Peggy Sue.
I have a boat that's blue.
We'll sail all day, and after that,
We'll have a barbecue.

The water feels so great.
Come over. Don't be late.
Bring your suit and flippers too.
I can hardly wait.

This rhyme includes words your child is working with in school: words with *ue* (*blue*) and words that end in a consonant + *er* (*water*). Together, find the words that rhyme with *Sue*. Look to see how the vowel sound is spelled for these words.

(fold here)

Name: _____

© Scott Foresman 2

You are your child's first and best teacher!

Here are ways to help your child practice skills while having fun!

Day 1   Use the following words with *ue* to create pairs of sentences that rhyme: *argue, avenue, barbecue, blue, clue, continue, due, glue, overdue, rescue, statue, tissue, true, untrue, value.*

Day 2   Your child is learning to read these words: *course, hear; things, which,* and *years.* Write these words on index cards. Have your child pick a word, read it aloud, and use it in a sentence.

Day 3   Take turns with your child pointing out interesting things you see as you walk or drive around your neighborhood. Each person gives one fact and one opinion about each object.

Day 4   Read a pararaph or a page from a nonfiction book with your child. Have your child listen for and identify the most important idea for the paragraph or page.

Day 5   Write the pronouns *I, you, she, he, we, they, me, her; him, us,* and *them* on separate index cards. Have your child choose cards and use the pronouns in sentences.

Read with your child EVERY DAY!

Kitchen Helpers

Materials crayons or markers, dictionary

Game Directions

1. Look at the kitchen scene. Take turns finding objects with names ending in the same sound you hear in *helper*. Possible answers are given below.

2. Write the names of the objects you find. Help your child use a dictionary to check the spellings of these names as needed.

3. The player who finds the most objects and writes them correctly wins!

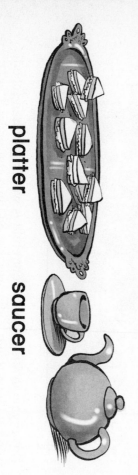

platter   **saucer**

Here are some of the objects you can find:

batter, butter, counter, dishwasher, electric beater, fire extinguisher, hamburger, pepper, pitcher, pot holder, stove burner, thermometer, timer, toaster, water

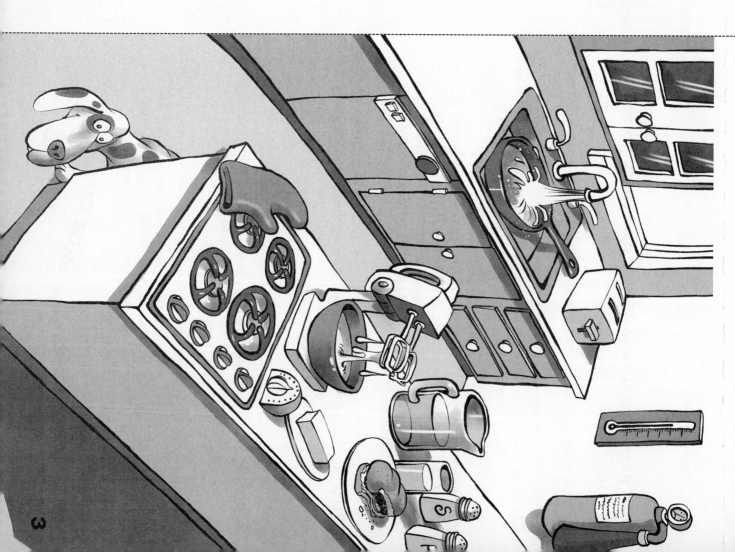

glue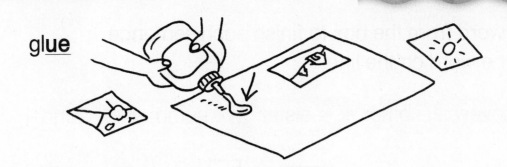

Pick a word from the box to match each clue.
Write the word on the line.

| avenue | blue | glue | rescue | statue | true |

1. save someone

_____

- - - - - - - - - - - - - - -

_____

2. a color

_____

- - - - - - - - - - - - - - -

_____

3. paste

_____

- - - - - - - - - - - - - - -

_____

4. not false

_____

- - - - - - - - - - - - - - -

_____

5.

_____

- - - - - - - - - - - - - - -

_____

6.

_____

- - - - - - - - - - - - - - -

_____

Notes for Home: Your child practiced reading and writing words in which the long *u* sound is spelled *ue*. **Home Activity:** Help your child use the words listed above in sentences.

© Scott Foresman 2

Pick a word from the box to finish each sentence.
Write the word on the line.

| never | other | sister | summer | under |

1. May is visiting New York this _____ .

2. Her _____ Becky is with her.

3. She has _____ been on a ferry before.

4. There are _____ boats on the bay.

5. The ferry goes _____ a bridge.

Notes for Home: Your child read and wrote words ending in *-er* with the same ending sound as *weather*. **Home Activity:** Help your child write a list of words that end in *-er* that describe types of people, such as *worker* or *skater*.

© Scott Foresman 2

Pick a word from the box to finish each sentence.
Write the word on the line.

| course | hear | things | which | years |

1. Jed and Matt have been sailing for two _____.

2. They know many _____ about sailing.

3. Their boat stays on its _____ .

4. They _____ cheers from the shore.

5. _____ sailboat do you think will win the race?

Notes for Home: This week your child is learning to read the words *course, hear, things, which,* and *years.* **Home Activity:** Have your child use some of these words in a broadcast about a made-up sports contest.

© Scott Foresman 2

Write F before each sentence that gives a **fact**.
Write O before each sentence that gives an **opinion**.

1. _____ I have been flying planes for ten years.

2. _____ I flew from New York to Texas today.

3. _____ I have a wonderful job.

4. _____ More people should fly rather than drive.

Write a fact about planes.

5. _____

_____

_____

Notes for Home: Your child practiced distinguishing between facts (statements that can be proven true or false) and opinions (statements that express a feeling or idea). *Home Activity:* As you read with your child, ask him or her to point out statements of fact and opinion.

© Scott Foresman 2

Some pronouns are used as subjects of sentences.
They are: **I, he, she, we, they.**

Some pronouns are used after action verbs.
They are: **me, him, her, us, them.**

Some pronouns can be used anywhere in a sentence.
They are: **you, it.**

Circle a pronoun to take the place of
the underlined word or words.

1. <u>My sisters and I</u> took Mike to the Statue of Liberty.

    We
    Us

2. Maria followed <u>Mike and me</u> inside.

    we
    us

3. Those stairs lead to the top of <u>the statue.</u>

    it
    you

4. <u>Mike</u> didn't want to climb the stairs.

    He
    Him

5. Julia and I followed <u>Maria</u> up the stairs.

    she
    her

Notes for Home: Your child chose pronouns to use as subjects or after action verbs. **Home Activity:** As you read to your child, point out nouns in sentences. Ask which pronouns he or she would use to replace these nouns.

© Scott Foresman 2

Pick a word from the box to match each clue.
Write the word on the line.

course   deck   dock   hear   steers   things   years

1. the floor of a ship   _____

2. the path of a boat   _____

3. a place to wait for a boat   _____

4. listen   _____

5. many, many months   _____

6. more than one thing   _____

7. drives   _____

Notes for Home: Your child used clues to practice new vocabulary words. **Home Activity:**
Pretend your child is the captain of a ship and you are a crew member. Use the vocabulary
words to act out a sea adventure.

© Scott Foresman 2

Name _____

Say the word for each picture.
Write a or **le** to finish each word.

People ride **a**cross the river.

I.

_____
bubb _____

2.

_____ wake

3.

_____
marb _____

4.

_____
app _____

Circle the words that have the same beginning sound as **across**.

5. after
alarm
ant

6. above
art
able

7. ate
arm
ahead

8. about
air
ash

Find the words that have the same ending sound as the picture.
Mark the space to show your answer.

9. ⬭ problem
⬭ purse
⬭ purple

10. ⬭ tumble
⬭ tumbling
⬭ telling

Notes for Home: Your child reviewed words that contain the schwa sound heard in *about* and *table*. **Home Activity:** Have your child read aloud some billboards and signs to you, pointing out words that contain the schwa sound.

© Scott Foresman 2

Name _____

| after | brother | flower | over | sister | summer |

Write four words from the box that begin with a consonant.

1. _____

2. _____

3. _____

4. _____

Write two words from the box that begin with a vowel.

5. _____

6. _____

Write two words from the box that are part of a family.

7. _____

8. _____

Pick a word from the box to finish each sentence.
Write the word on the line.

| year | which |

9. Last _____ we went on a ferry to the city.

10. _____ city did you visit?

Notes for Home: Your child spelled words that end in -er and two frequently used words: year, which. **Home Activity:** Write these words on slips of paper. Have your child draw two slips and write a sentence trying to use both words.

Name _____

Circle a pronoun to use in place of the underlined word or words.

1. <u>Kim</u> lives on a boat called a sampan.

She
Her

2. Other families live in boats near <u>Kim's family</u>.

they
them

3. <u>Her mother and father</u> catch fish.

They
Them

4. Kim helps take care of <u>her little brother</u>.

he
him

I	she	he	we	they	you
me	her	him	us	them	it

Use at least one word from the box.
Write a sentence about something you can ride.

_____

- -

5. _____

Notes for Home: Your child reviewed subject pronouns *(I, she, he, we, they, you, it)* and object pronouns *(me, her, him, us, them, you, it)*. **Home Activity:** Write these pronouns on index cards. Take turns picking a word and using it in a sentence.

© Scott Foresman 2

Test-Taking Tips

1. Write your name on the test.

2. Read each question twice.

3. Read all the answer choices for the question.

4. Mark your answer carefully.

5. Check your answer.

© Scott Foresman 2

Name _____

Part 1: Vocabulary

Find the word that best fits in each sentence.
Mark the space for your answer.

1. Mr. Brown _____ the boat.
   - ⬭ says
   - ⬭ steers
   - ⬭ rockets

2. Neena's sister is three _____ old.
   - ⬭ years
   - ⬭ feathers
   - ⬭ crops

3. We walked on the _____ of the ship.
   - ⬭ course
   - ⬭ deck
   - ⬭ oven

4. Please put your _____ away.
   - ⬭ things
   - ⬭ paws
   - ⬭ years

5. Bill jumped off the _____ into the water.
   - ⬭ world
   - ⬭ country
   - ⬭ dock

© Scott Foresman 2

GO ON ➡

Part 2: Comprehension

Read each question.
Mark the space for your answer.

6. This story is mostly about —
   - ⬯ the Statue of Liberty.
   - ⬯ New York City.
   - ⬯ Captain Cruz.

7. Captain Cruz's ferry is for —
   - ⬯ animals.
   - ⬯ people.
   - ⬯ cars.

8. A captain's log is a kind of —
   - ⬯ book.
   - ⬯ tree.
   - ⬯ rope.

9. Captain Cruz is a good captain because —
   - ⬯ a helper sits beside him.
   - ⬯ he likes his job.
   - ⬯ he keeps everyone safe.

10. Which sentence is an opinion?
    - ⬯ "Captain Cruz uses a radio."
    - ⬯ "The captain does his job well."
    - ⬯ "That's Mr. Cruz, my neighbor."

STOP

© Scott Foresman 2

Name _____

birds

 benches

Say the word for each picture.
Add -s or **-es** to finish each word.

1.	2.	3.	4.
nose ___	dish ___	box ___	walrus ___

5.	6.	7.	8.
horse ___	face ___	brush ___	rose ___

Find the word that names only one.
Mark the space to show your answer.

9. ⬭ glass
   ⬭ places
   ⬭ porches

10. ⬭ foxes
    ⬭ mess
    ⬭ spaces

Notes for Home: Your child reviewed adding -s or -es to nouns to show more than one.
Home Activity: Have your child read aloud each word above with and without the
-s or -es ending. Ask your child how many syllables are in each word.

© Scott Foresman 2

Name _____

after   brother   flower   over   sister   summer

Change one or two letters in each word to make a word from the box.
Write the new word on the line.

1. mister

_____

2. offer

_____

3. oven

_____

4. supper

_____

5. slower

_____

6. mother

_____

Write the word from the box that has the same beginning sound as the picture.

year   which

7.

_____

8.

_____

Notes for Home: Your child spelled words that end in *-er* and two frequently used words: *year, which.* **Home Activity:** Write each spelling word with its letters scrambled. Ask your child to unscramble and write each word.

© Scott Foresman 2

Family Times

Splash!

Down in the Sea: The Jelly Fish

My Wonderful Neighborhood

In my wonderful neighborhood under the sea
Live eight beige clams smiling right at me.
There's an octopus going on a shopping spree
In my wonderful neighborhood under the sea.

In my wonderful neighborhood under the sea
There's one pointy starfish floating gracefully.
There's a really big lobster weighing more than me
In my wonderful neighborhood under the sea.

This rhyme includes words your child is working with in school: words with the long *a* sound spelled *ei* as in *eight*, and words that have added endings and suffixes like *smiling* and *wonderful*. Sing the rhyme together. Help your child read and say the words with more than one syllable.

(fold here)

Name: _____

© Scott Foresman 2

You are your child's first and best teacher!

Here are ways to help your child practice skills while having fun!

Day 1 Write each of the following words in a list: *beige, eight, freight, neigh, neighbor, rein, reindeer, sleigh, veil, weigh, weight.* Help your child draw pictures and write captions for them using these words.

Day 2 Encourage your child to use the words *cold, grow, most, move,* and *near* to make up a song or poem about living under the sea.

Day 3 Look through a magazine or newspaper with your child for maps, tables, graphs, and pictures. Discuss what information each graphic source shows.

Day 4 Your child is practicing speaking clearly and politely on the telephone. Act out telephone conversations with your child to practice calling and asking for information, such as how late the library stays open.

Day 5 Find out more about underwater sea life. Help your child take notes on some of the information you find. Encourage your child to use to these notes when telling someone else about this topic.

Read with your child EVERY 1

Underwater Walk

Materials paper circle, paper clip, pencil, 1 coin, 1 button per player, game board

Game Directions

1. Make a simple spinner as shown.

2. Players take turns tossing a coin and moving one space for heads and two spaces for tails.

3. Players then spin the spinner and add the word ending to the word on the gameboard to try to make a new word, if possible. If a word can't be made, the player goes back to his or her previous position.

4. The first player to get to the end wins!

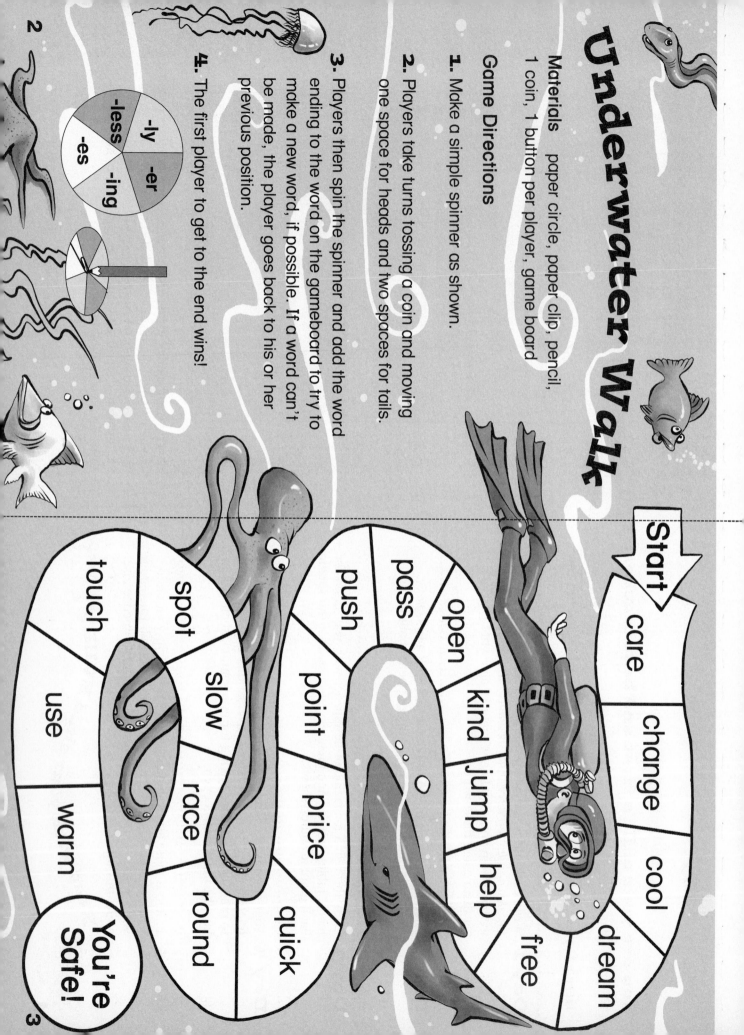

Spinner: -ly, -er, -ing, -es, -less

Start

care — change — cool — dream — free

open — kind — jump — help

pass — push

point — price — quick — round

spot — slow — race

touch — use — warm

You're Safe!

2

3

Name _____

Pick the word that has the **long a** sound.
Write the word on the line.

fr**ei**ght train

1.
   piece
   weigh
   artichoke

   _____
   -
   _____

2.
   talks
   neighbors
   friends

   _____
   -
   _____

3.
   neigh
   nag
   niece

   _____
   -
   _____

4. **8**
   eat
   eight
   candle

   _____
   -
   _____

5.
   veil
   head
   bride

   _____
   -
   _____

6.
   sleigh
   field
   sled

   _____
   -
   _____

7.
   head
   animal
   reins

   _____
   -
   _____

8.
   deer
   antlers
   reindeer

   _____
   -
   _____

Notes for Home: Your child wrote words in which the long *a* sound is spelled *ei*. **Home Activity:** List these word pairs: *weigh-way, rein-rain,* and *eight-ate.* Have your child read these words and use them in sentences.

© Scott Foresman 2

Circle a word to finish each sentence.

1. Many big fish like to eat sea _____ .

    horses
    horsing

2. A sea horse is not a very good _____ .

    swimmer
    swimming

3. It has small fins so it swims very _____ .

    slower
    slowly

4. It moves by _____ the waves.

    rider
    riding

5. It _____ its color to hide.

    changing
    changes

Notes for Home: Your child read words in which adding endings such as *-ly, -less,* or *-ing* adds syllables *(quick, quickly).* **Home Activity:** Look at the words above. Discuss how the sound and meaning of words change when endings are added *(care, careless, caring).*

134 **Phonics: Words with Endings and Suffixes**

Level 2.2

© Scott Foresman 2

Pick a word from the box to finish each sentence.
Write the word on the line. Use each word only once.

| cold | grow | most | move | near |

1. _____ seals live in the sea.

2. Some spend time on _____ chunks of ice.

3. Seal pups _____ slowly on land.

4. They stay _____ their mothers.

5. They _____ up fast.

Notes for Home: This week your child is learning to read the words *cold, grow, most, move,* and *near.* **Home Activity:** Have your child use some of these words to write a conversation between two animals that live in the sea.

© Scott Foresman 2

Name _____

Read the sentences. **Look** at the pictures.
Answer the questions.

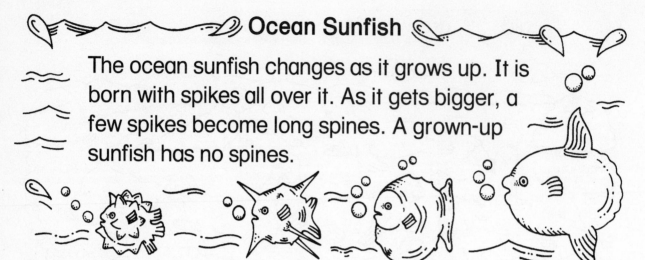

Ocean Sunfish

The ocean sunfish changes as it grows up. It is born with spikes all over it. As it gets bigger, a few spikes become long spines. A grown-up sunfish has no spines.

A. Soon after hatching   **B.** Growing up   **C.** Nearly grown up   **D.** All grown up

I. A baby sunfish has many spikes. What happens to them as the sunfish grows up?

_____

- -

_____

2. Look at picture B.
How many long spikes does the sunfish have? _____

3. How is the fish in picture D different from the fish in picture C?

_____

- -

_____

- -

_____

Notes for Home: Your child has been learning about looking at graphics, such as diagrams and charts, in order to better understand text. **Home Activity:** Check out library books that use graphics to give information. Discuss with your child the purpose of each graphic.

© Scott Foresman 2

A **pronoun** takes the place of a noun or nouns. When you use pronouns, you don't need to use the same noun over and over.

Pick a pronoun from the box to finish the second sentence. Use each word only once. **Circle** the word or words in the first sentence that helped you decide which pronoun to use.

| he | it | she | them | they |

1. John took us to a tide pool. There _____ showed us a mole crab.

2. This crab has long feelers.

   It uses _____ to catch food.

3. My sister picked up a stick.

   Then _____ poked it in the sand.

4. Suddenly, all we saw was sand.

   The crab was hidden under _____ .

5. My sister and I saw two tiny bumps.

   John told us that _____ were its eyes.

Notes for Home: For each pair of sentences, your child replaced nouns with pronouns. *Home Activity:* Have your child pretend that he or she is visiting the bottom of the sea. Ask him or her to write you a postcard from there using several pronouns.

© Scott Foresman 2

Name _____

Pick a word from the box to match each clue.
Write the word on the line. Use each word only once.

beach	cold	floating	flopped
grow	move	near	poke

1.

_____

- - - - - - - - - - - - - - - -

_____

2.

_____

- - - - - - - - - - - - - - - -

_____

3. close by

_____

- - - - - - - - - - - - - - - -

_____

4. get bigger

_____

- - - - - - - - - - - - - - - -

_____

5. jab

_____

- - - - - - - - - - - - - - - -

_____

6. The fish _____ on the deck.

_____

- - - - - - - - - - - - - - - -

_____

7. not hot

_____

- - - - - - - - - - - - - - - -

_____

8. go to a new place

_____

- - - - - - - - - - - - - - - -

_____

Notes for Home: Your child used word and picture clues to practice new vocabulary words.
Home Activity: Have your child use some of these words to tell you a story about a morning on a beach.

© Scott Foresman 2

Circle the word that has the same vowel sound as cl<u>ue</u>.
Write the word on the line.

1. glue   glee   glad
_____

2. avenue   about   above
_____

3. scrub   rescue   stuff
_____

4. trust   trouble   threw
_____

5. true   trip   trouble
_____

6. blush   blue   blur
_____

7. bark   barbecue   butter
_____

8. grape   grew   grain
_____

Find the picture that has the same vowel sound as **blue**.
Mark the space to show your answer.

9. ⬭   ⬭   ⬭

10. ⬭   ⬭   ⬭

Notes for Home: Your child reviewed words spelled with *ue* that have the vowel sound heard in *statue*. **Home Activity:** Write sentences using the words *Sue, blue, clue, glue,* and *true*. Help your child read them. Ask your child to draw pictures to match the sentences.

© Scott Foresman 2

| neighbor | reindeer | sleigh | veil | weigh | weight |

Write four words from the box that have the **long a** sound spelled **eigh**.

1. _____

2. _____

3. _____

4. _____

Write two words from the box that have the **long a** sound spelled **ei**.

5. _____

6. _____

Write the two words from the box that rhyme.

7. _____

8. _____

Read the first letter of each word in each sentence.
Write the letters on the line to make a word from the box.

grow
near

9. Nine elks are returning. _____

10. Get roses or weeds. _____

Notes for Home: Your child spelled words in which the long *a* sound is spelled *ei (veil)* and *eigh (weight)* and two frequently used words: *grow, near*. **Home Activity:** Say each spelling word aloud. Have your child repeat the word and spell it.

© Scott Foresman 2

Circle a word to finish each sentence.
Write the word on the line.

She   Her

1. _____ sees the seals.

He   Him   he   him

2. _____ gives _____ a book.

They   Them

3. _____ watch one seal eat.

we   us

4. "Is the seal looking at _____?"

I   me

5. "The seal is feeding _____!"

Notes for Home: Your child practiced using pronouns in sentences. *Home Activity:* Encourage your child to use pronouns to write about something that happened in school this week.

© Scott Foresman   2

Test-Taking Tips

1. Write your name on the test.

2. Read each question twice.

3. Read all the answer choices for the question.

4. Mark your answer carefully.

5. Check your answer.

© Scott Foresman 2

Part I: Vocabulary

Find the word that best fits in each sentence.
Mark the space for your answer.

1. Plants need water and sun to _____ .
   ⬭ trade   ⬭ keep   ⬭ grow

2. When you _____ me, it hurts.
   ⬭ poke   ⬭ follow   ⬭ beach

3. Will you sit _____ me today?
   ⬭ near   ⬭ still   ⬭ between

4. A log was _____ in the water.
   ⬭ sealing   ⬭ floating   ⬭ dashing

5. The dog _____ down on the grass.
   ⬭ drew   ⬭ flopped   ⬭ gathered

© Scott Foresman 2

GO ON ➡

Part 2: Comprehension

Read each question.

Mark the space for your answer.

6. Many of the jellyfish in this story look like —
   - ⬭ wheels.
   - ⬭ ducks.
   - ⬭ parachutes.

7. Most jellyfish use tentacles to —
   - ⬭ catch food.
   - ⬭ swim.
   - ⬭ walk.

8. What will happen if you poke a jellyfish?
   - ⬭ It will melt.
   - ⬭ It will sting you.
   - ⬭ It will eat your finger.

9. The writer wanted to —
   - ⬭ give facts about jellyfish.
   - ⬭ tell how to catch a jellyfish.
   - ⬭ show that jellyfish are not really fish.

10. Which sentence is an opinion?
   - ⬭ Jellyfish eat fish, crabs, and worms.
   - ⬭ Each jellyfish lives about a year.
   - ⬭ Jellyfish are pretty.

STOP

© Scott Foresman 2

Say the word for each picture.
Write the word on the line.
Use the words in the box if you need help.

baker	camper	catcher
marcher	mother	teacher

sing**er**

1.

_____

2.

_____

3.

_____

4.

_____

5.

_____

6.

_____

Find the word that has the same ending sound as the picture.
Mark the space to show your answer.

7. ⬭ very
   ⬭ here
   ⬭ after

8. ⬭ weather
   ⬭ year
   ⬭ somewhere

Notes for Home: Your child reviewed words ending in *-er* that have the schwa sound heard in *singer*. **Home Activity:** Many words ending in *-er* name people who do things, such as *singer*. Work with your child to list other words like this.

Phonics: Consonant + *er* Review

© Scott Foresman 2

| neighbor | reindeer | sleigh | veil | weigh | weight |

Write a word from the box that sounds the same as the word or words below.

1. way _____

_____

2. wait _____

_____

Pick a word from the box to match each clue.
Write the word on the line.

3. rain + dear _____

_____

4. like a sled _____

_____

5. It is what a bride wears. _____

_____

6. It is someone who lives near you. _____

Write the word from the box that means the opposite of each word below.

grow   near

7. far _____

_____

8. shrink _____

_____

Notes for Home: Your child spelled words in which the long *a* sound is spelled *ei* (v*ei*l) and *eigh* (w*eigh*t) and two frequently used words: *grow, near.* **Home Activity:** Encourage your child to draw a snowy scene and to use the spelling words to write about the picture.

© Scott Foresman 2

Family Times

Tex and the Big Bad T. Rex

Let's Go Dinosaur Tracking!

Exercise with Dino!

Exercise with Dino.
He'll show you how.
Express yourself!
And flex right now!

Discover your strength.
Do an extra hop.
Uncurl your tail.
Next you can stop.

Replay the song.
Redo each move.
Exercise with Dino.
Move to the groove!

This rhyme includes words your child is working with in school: words with *ex (extra)* and words that begin with the prefixes *un-, dis-,* and *re-.* Read "Exercise with Dino" aloud with your child. Hop each time you say a word with *ex.* Clap for each word with the prefix *un-, dis-,* or *re-.*

(fold here)

Name: _____

© Scott Foresman 2

You are your child's first and best teacher!

Here are ways to help your child practice skills while having fun!

Day 1 Help your child think of words that have the letter combination *ex* in them such as *next* or *Texas.* Write a list of these words.

Day 2 Your child is learning to read the words *along, front, probably, right,* and *someday.* Use these words during a conversation about a future family trip.

Day 3 Read a nonfiction story or news article with your child. As you read, pause to ask your child to tell you the main idea of a paragraph or page.

Day 4 Have your child search a story for word pairs that can be rewritten as contractions, such as *is not (isn't)* or *it is (it's).* Help your child write these contractions.

Day 5 Your child is learning to use proper grammar when speaking. Help correct any incorrect uses of language you hear by asking: *Does that sound right to you? Is that the correct word to use?*

Read with your child

Adding Prefixes

Materials paper circle, paper clip, pencil, 1 button per player, game board

Game Directions

1. Make a simple spinner as shown.

2. Take turns spinning to get a prefix, and then tossing a button on the gameboard. Players try to make a new word, if possible, by adding the prefix to the word landed on.

3. Players earn 1 point for each new word. Use a word only once. Make a list to keep track of words used.

4. The first player to earn 5 points wins!

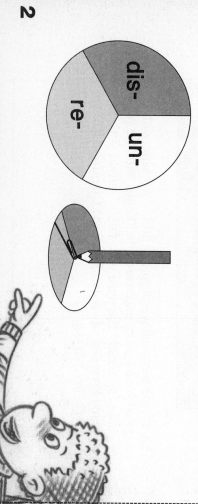

paint	write	lock	cover	happy
appear	wind	do	obey	pack
agree	fill	wrap	tie	honest
trust	loyal	lucky	pay	read
kind	build	safe	make	like

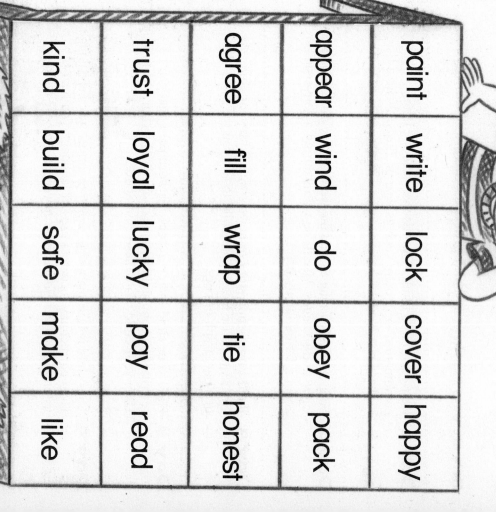

Name _____

Pick a word from the box to finish each sentence.
Write the word on the line. Use each word only once.

| next | excited | expert | extra | explain |

Texas

1. Dr. Sanchez is an _____ on dinosaurs.

2. Her books _____ how dinosaurs lived.

3. I can't wait for her _____ book about them.

4. I am _____ about going to hear her talk tonight.

5. I have an _____ ticket if you want to come!

Notes for Home: Your child read and wrote words that contain the letter combination *ex*.
Home Activity: Help your child make up facts about someone named Rex, using a word
containing *ex* in each sentence, for example: *Rex is an expert swimmer.*

© Scott Foresman 2

Read each clue.

Add un-, dis-, or **re-** to the word to match each clue.

Hint: Adding **un-** or **dis-** makes a word mean the opposite.

Adding **re-** makes it mean "do again."

happy   **un**happy

1. not lucky

   _____

   - - - - - - - -
   _____ lucky

2. paint again

   _____

   - - - - - - - -
   _____ paint

3. not agree

   _____

   - - - - - - - -
   _____ agree

4. opposite of *pack*

   _____

   - - - - - - - -
   _____ pack

5. not locked

   _____

   - - - - - - - -
   _____ locked

6. build again

   _____

   - - - - - - - -
   _____ build

7. not obey

   _____

   - - - - - - - -
   _____ obey

8. not safe

   _____

   - - - - - - - -
   _____ safe

9. read again

   _____

   - - - - - - - -
   _____ read

10. not honest

   _____

   - - - - - - - -
   _____ honest

Notes for Home: Your child practiced figuring out the meanings of words with the prefixes *un-, dis-,* and *re-*. **Home Activity:** Look for words like these in ads and signs. Help your child pronounce these words and figure out what they mean.

© Scott Foresman 2

Circle a word to finish each sentence.

1. This dinosaur had very short _____ legs.

right
front

2. It moved _____ on its hind legs.

along
front

3. It was _____ a very scary creature.

probably
someday

4. I knew _____ away I wouldn't want to meet one.

along
right

5. _____ I'd like to dig up dinosaur bones.

Someday
Right

Notes for Home: This week your child is learning to read the words *along, front, probably, right,* and *someday.* **Home Activity:** Have your child use some of these words to write a news announcement about an imaginary and interesting discovery.

© Scott Foresman 2

Name _____

Read the paragraph.

Most reptiles lay their eggs and walk away. Scientists thought dinosaurs were like reptiles. Now some scientists think the dinosaur parents were there when the eggs hatched. They may have fed their babies. They may have kept them safe from harm. Perhaps dinosaurs were good parents after all.

1. Write a sentence that tells the main idea of the paragraph.

_____

- -

_____

- -

_____

2. Draw a picture that shows the main idea.

3. Write a title for the paragraph.

_____

- -

_____

Notes for Home: Your child found the most important idea of a paragraph. *Home Activity:* Read aloud paragraphs from a nature magazine or book to your child. Stop to talk about what the most important idea is in each paragraph.

© Scott Foresman 2

Name _____

A **contraction** is a word made by putting two words together. An **apostrophe** , shows where letters have been left out.

We **will see** the dinosaurs.
We'll see the dinosaurs.

Put the words together to make a contraction.
Write the contraction on the line.

1. is not

   _____
   - - - - - - - - - -
   _____

2. we are

   _____
   - - - - - - - - - -
   _____

3. he is

   _____
   - - - - - - - - - -
   _____

4. we have

   _____
   - - - - - - - - - -
   _____

5. they are

   _____
   - - - - - - - - - -
   _____

6. do not

   _____
   - - - - - - - - - -
   _____

Pick a word from the box to finish each sentence.
Write the word on the line.

aren't   haven't

7. There _____ any dinosaurs alive today.

8. They _____ been here for millions of years.

© Scott Foresman 2

Notes for Home: Your child wrote contractions by joining a pronoun and a verb or a verb with the word *not*. **Home Activity:** As you read, point out contractions. Have your child write the two words that were used to make each contraction.

Pick a word from the box to match each clue.
Write the word on the line.

claws	front	giant	helmet
probably	someday	stone	right

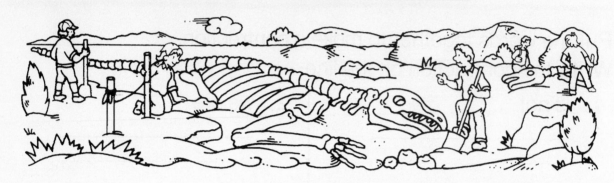

1. huge

_____

- - - - - - - - - - - - - - - -

_____

2. a day in the future

_____

- - - - - - - - - - - - - - - -

_____

3. not back

_____

- - - - - - - - - - - - - - - -

_____

4. Do it _____ away!

_____

- - - - - - - - - - - - - - - -

_____

5. a hard hat

_____

- - - - - - - - - - - - - - - -

_____

6. a rock

_____

- - - - - - - - - - - - - - - -

_____

7. a crab's "hands"

_____

- - - - - - - - - - - - - - - -

_____

8. likely

_____

- - - - - - - - - - - - - - - -

_____

Notes for Home: Your child used word and picture clues to practice new vocabulary words.
Home Activity: Encourage your child to use these words to tell a fantasy story about a giant
dinosaur or dragon with big claws.

© Scott Foresman 2

eight

Each word pair goes with the picture.
Circle the word that has the same **long a** sound as **eight**.
Write the word on the line.

1.

weigh   apple
_____
- - - - - - - - - - - - - - - -

2.

neighbor   talk
_____
- - - - - - - - - - - - - - - -

3.

reindeer   antler
_____
- - - - - - - - - - - - - - - -

4.

sleigh   dash
_____
- - - - - - - - - - - - - - - -

5.

hair   veil
_____
- - - - - - - - - - - - - - - -

6.

reins   saddle
_____
- - - - - - - - - - - - - - - -

Find the word that has the same vowel sound as the picture.
Mark the space to show your answer.

7. ⬭ grass
⬭ beige
⬭ taps

8. ⬭ weight
⬭ white
⬭ whole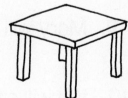

Notes for Home: Your child reviewed words with the long *a* sound spelled *ei* as heard in *eight*. **Home Activity:** Write the words with *ei* listed above on slips of paper. Take turns drawing words and using each word in a sentence.

© Scott Foresman 2

| undo | unfair | unhappy | unlike | unlucky | untie |

Write four words from the box that have two syllables.

1. _____

2. _____

3. _____

4. _____

Write two words from the box that have three syllables.

5. _____

6. _____

Pick a word from the box to match each clue.
Write the word on the line.

7. not glad

_____

8. not the same

_____

Pick a word from the box to finish each sentence.
Write the word on the line.

| front | probably |

9. Mary will _____ come to the show.

10. We will sit in the _____ row.

Notes for Home: Your child spelled words that begin with the prefix *un-* and two frequently used words: *front, probably.* **Home Activity:** Help your child write a clue for each word with *un-*. Discuss how this prefix changes the meaning of a word.

© Scott Foresman 2

Name _____

Take out sentences that don't belong with the other sentences in a paragraph.

    Dinosaurs lived a long time ago. They were the largest animals on Earth then. ~~You can see dinosaur bones today~~. Some dinosaurs were bigger than houses. Anklyosaurus could be up to 56 feet long!

Read the sentences.

Pick three sentences that belong together.

Draw a line through the one that doesn't belong.

1. Ankylosaurus looked a little like a turtle.
2. That is because it had a hard shell like a turtle.
3. Turtles are very slow animals.
4. However, Ankylosaurus was much larger than a turtle.

Write three sentences that belong together about dinosaurs.

5. _____

_____

_____

_____

_____

_____

Notes for Home: Your child identified and wrote sentences that belong together.
Home Activity: Copy a few sentences each from several paragraphs of a story and cut them up. Have your child group the sentences that make sense together.

© Scott Foresman 2

Use the words in ( ) to make a contraction.
Write the contraction on the line to finish each sentence.

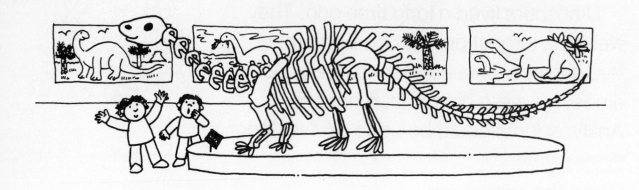

_____ (had not)
- - - - - - - - - - - - - - - - - - - -

1. They _____ seen a dinosaur before.

_____ (It is)
- - - - - - - - - - - - - - - - - - -

2. _____ much bigger than an elephant.

_____ (They are)
- - - - - - - - - - - - - - - - - - -

3. _____ glad to see this one.

_____ (would not)
- - - - - - - - - - - - - - - - -

4. They _____ like to meet a live one.

_____ (They will)
- - - - - - - - - - - - - - - -

5. _____ dream of dinosaurs tonight.

Notes for Home: Your child wrote contractions. *Home Activity:* Read with your child and point out pairs of words that can be made into contractions. Have him or her write the contractions and reread the sentences with the contractions in place.

© Scott Foresman 2

Part 1: Vocabulary

Find the word that best fits in each sentence.
Mark the space for your answer.

1. Jason puts on a _____ when he rides his bike.
   - ⬭ surface
   - ⬭ helmet
   - ⬭ someday

2. The bear's _____ are sharp.
   - ⬭ claws
   - ⬭ rockets
   - ⬭ tools

3. The wall was made of _____ .
   - ⬭ giant
   - ⬭ stone
   - ⬭ beach

4. Mina lost her _____ tooth.
   - ⬭ front
   - ⬭ word
   - ⬭ poke

5. We will _____ go to the zoo.
   - ⬭ since
   - ⬭ should
   - ⬭ probably

© Scott Foresman 2

GO ON ➡️

Part 2: Comprehension

Read each question.
Mark the space for your answer.

6. What happened first?
   - ⬭ The tracks turned to stone.
   - ⬭ A dinosaur left some tracks.
   - ⬭ Sand covered the tracks.

7. This story is mostly about —
   - ⬭ finding a real dinosaur.
   - ⬭ Roland Bird.
   - ⬭ looking for dinosaur tracks.

8. You can tell that sauropods were —
   - ⬭ very large.
   - ⬭ three-legged.
   - ⬭ meat eaters.

9. What did you learn about dinosaurs from this story?
   - ⬭ Most dinosaurs were shaped like birds.
   - ⬭ There were many different kinds.
   - ⬭ All dinosaurs were very large.

10. Where is the best place to look for dinosaur tracks?
    - ⬭ in a field of grass
    - ⬭ in a lake
    - ⬭ on flat stone

STOP

© Scott Foresman 2

Circle a word to finish each sentence.

1. It looks around _____ .

   careless carefully caring

2. It is a fast _____ .

   running runny runner

3. It is _____ .

   helper helpful helpless

4. It is _____ .

   sleepless sleepy sleeper

Find the words that mean "glad" or "gladly."
Mark the spaces to show your answers.

5. ⬭ sleepy
   ⬭ happily
   ⬭ tired

6. ⬭ cheerful
   ⬭ sadly
   ⬭ slowly

Notes for Home: Your child reviewed words with more than one syllable that end in *-er, -ing, -less, -ful, -ly,* and *-y.* **Home Activity:** Work with your child to list some other words with these endings. Together, write a silly poem about dinosaurs with the words from your list.

© Scott Foresman 2

undo   unfair   unhappy   unlike   unlucky   untie

Add un- to each word to make a word from the box.
Write the new word on the line.

1. do

_____

- - - - - - - - - - - - - - - -

_____

2. happy

_____

- - - - - - - - - - - - - - - -

_____

3. tie

_____

- - - - - - - - - - - - - - - -

_____

4. lucky

_____

- - - - - - - - - - - - - - - -

_____

5. like

_____

- - - - - - - - - - - - - - - -

_____

6. fair

_____

- - - - - - - - - - - - - - - -

_____

Pick a word from the box to match
each clue.
Write the word on the line.

front   probably

_____

- - - - - - - - - - - - - - - -

7. likely _____

_____

- - - - - - - - - - - - - - - -

8. opposite of *back* _____

Notes for Home: Your child spelled words with the prefix *un-* and two frequently used
words: *front, probably.* **Home Activity:** Help your child make crossword puzzles that include
these spelling words. Work together to think of clues for each word.

© Scott Foresman 2

Correct each sentence.
Write it on the line.
Hint: Check that all pronouns are used correctly.

1. Me wrote a report on dinosaurs.

_____
_____
_____

2. Them were big animals.

_____
_____

3. Mrs. Lee said he liked it.

_____
_____

4. Her liked my pictures.

_____
_____

5. My dad was proud of I.

_____
_____
_____

 Notes for Home: Your child corrected pronouns in sentences. *Home Activity:* Read a story together. Look for sentences with nouns that can be replaced with pronouns. Have your child read the sentences using the proper pronouns. (*Mike* threw the ball. *He* threw it.)

© Scott Foresman 2

Words I Can Now Read and Write

© Scott Foresman 2

Family Times

The Clubhouse

Lemonade for Sale

Let's Build a Clubhouse

Let's build a clubhouse. What shall we do?
First we need some money,
Then some help from you!
We'll have a bake sale here tonight.
We'll bake some cookies
So they taste just right.
We'll bake a cake and sell each piece.
Please pay Shirley and her little niece.
Half of the money we'll give away.
Half of the money we'll save today.
We'll take a photograph of our bake sale.
We'll hang the photo
On a little nail!

This rhyme includes words your child is working with in school: words with the long *e* sound spelled *ie* and *ey* (*piece, money*) and words with *ph* and *lf* (*photograph, half*). Read the rhyme with your child. Circle all the long *e* words spelled *ie* and *ey*. Underline the words with *ph* and *lf*.

(fold here)

Name: _____

© Scott Foresman 2

You are your child's first and best teacher!

Here are ways to help your child practice skills while having fun!

Day 1 Write a list of words with long *e* spelled *ie* and *ey* such as *chief, cookie, piece, money, monkey,* and *honey.* Use some of these long *e* words to help your child write a story about a monkey.

Day 2 Take turns making up sentences that include these words that your child is learning to read: *above, few, kept, number, sound.*

Day 3 After you read a story with your child, discuss which parts of the story could really happen and which parts are make-believe.

Day 4 Have your child make a poster that advertises a food that he or she likes. Encourage your child to include information that tells his or her opinion about the product.

Day 5 Ask your child what makes a good listener and a good speaker. Then talk with your child about his or her day to practice these listening and speaking skills.

Read with your child EVERY DAY!

Climb a Tree

Materials 1 coin, 1 button per player, game board

Game Directions

1. Each player chooses a tree to climb.

2. Players take turns flipping a coin. Move one space for heads and two spaces for tails.

3. As each player lands on a word, he or she reads it aloud and uses it in a sentence. If a player cannot read the word or use it in a sentence correctly, the player moves back to his or her previous position.

4. The first player to reach the top wins!

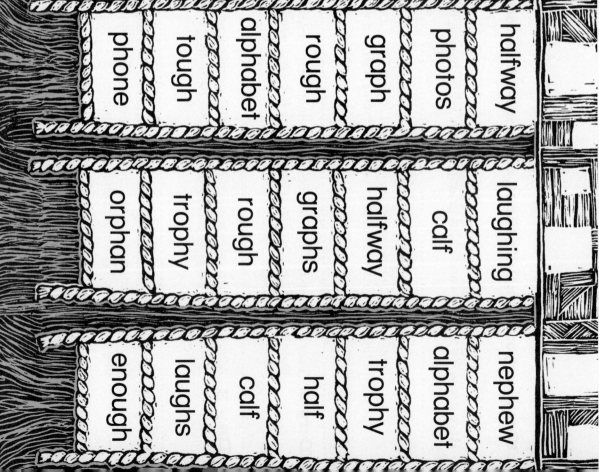

halfway	laughing	nephew
photos	calf	alphabet
graph	halfway	trophy
rough	graphs	half
alphabet	rough	calf
tough	trophy	laughs
phone	orphan	enough

Name _____

Say the word for each picture.
Write ie or **ey** to finish each word.
Use the words in the box if you need help.

th**ie**f   key

| briefcase | chief | cookie | honey |
| money | monkey | piece | turkey |

1.

ch _____ f

2.

cook _____

3.

p _____ ce

4.

hon _____

5.

monk _____

6.

turk _____

7.

mon _____

8.

br _____ fcase

 Notes for Home: Your child wrote words with the long *e* sound spelled *ie* and *ey* as in *thief* and *key*. **Home Activity:** Work with your child to write a story using as many of the pictured words as possible.

© Scott Foresman 2

Name _____

Pick the word that has the same consonant sound heard at the end of **graph**.

Write the word on the line to finish each sentence.

gra**ph**

---

enough   some

1. Did we make _____ ?

---

up   halfway

2. It is filled _____ .

---

cough   sneeze

3. Don't _____ , please.

---

trophy   medal

4. We deserve a _____ .

---

smile   laugh

5. Don't _____ , it's true.

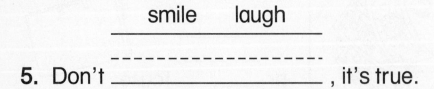

Notes for Home: Your child finished sentences using words with the consonants *gh*, *ph*, and *lf* that represent the sound /f/. **Home Activity:** Make up rhymes with your child using the words with *gh*, *ph*, and *lf* shown above.

© Scott Foresman 2

Draw a line to match each word to a clue.

1. above

2. few

3. kept

4. number

5. sound

a. something you hear

b. not below

c. not many

d. tells how many

e. the opposite of "gave away"

Write a sentence for each word in the box on the lines below.

| above | few | kept | number | sound |

6. _____

7. _____

8. _____

9. _____

10. _____

Notes for Home: This week your child is learning to read the words *above, few, kept, number,* and *sound.* **Home Activity:** Have your child tell you about an experience buying or selling something using as many of the listed words as possible.

© Scott Foresman 2

Name _____

Look at each picture.
Circle R if the picture shows something that could really happen.
Circle F if the picture shows something that could not really happen.

1.   R   F

2.   R   F

3.   R   F

4.   R   F

5.   R   F

6.   R   F

7.   R   F

8.   R   F

9.   R   F

Draw a picture of something that could happen in a fantasy.
10.

Notes for Home: Your child identified things that could happen in a realistic story and things that could happen in a fantasy. **Home Activity:** Read a story. Ask your child to identify realistic events (real people doing ordinary things) and fantasy events (animals talking).

© Scott Foresman 2

Name _____

A **sentence** is a group of words that tell a complete idea.

Sentence: Toby likes to drink lemonade.
Not a sentence: A hot and thirsty Toby.

Read the words.
Write an **S** on the line if the words are a complete sentence.
Write an **N** on the line if the words are **not** a complete sentence.

_____ 1. Chris has a plan.

_____ 2. Wants to sell.

_____ 3. I love lemonade and cookies!

_____ 4. More cookies.

Write a sentence to go with the picture above.

5. _____

Notes for Home: Your child identified and wrote complete sentences. *Home Activity:* Ask your child to tell you a story about solving a problem. Encourage him or her to use complete sentences.

© Scott Foresman 2

Level 2.2

Grammar: Complete Sentences 171

Name _____

Pick a word from the box to finish each sentence.
Write the word on the line.

above	few	ice	kept
lemonade	number	sound	

1. Did you hear that _____ ?

2. It came from _____ us.

3. There are a _____ lemons in the tree.

4. Let's count the _____ of lemons.

5. Let's make _____ to drink.

6. Mom _____ the lemons we picked.

7. We need _____ to make it cold.

Notes for Home: Your child completed sentences using words that he or she learned to read this week. **Home Activity:** Work with your child to write a story using as many of these words as possible. Read the story aloud to other family members or friends.

© Scott Foresman 2

Name _____

Use the graphs to answer the questions.

Cups of Lemonade Sold

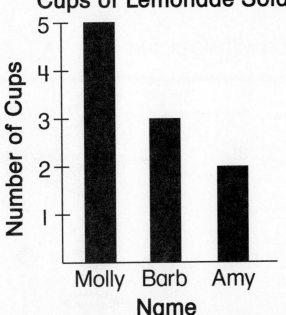

Cups of Lemonade Sold

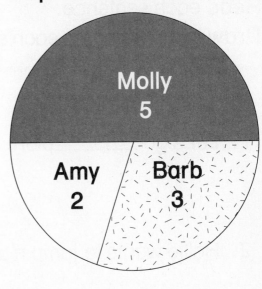

1. What do the graphs show?

_____

- -

_____

2. Who sold the most cups of lemonade? _____

3. Who sold the fewest cups of lemonade? _____

4. How many cups were sold all together? _____

5. Which graph is easier for you to read? Why?

_____

- -

_____

Notes for Home: Your child compared information on a circle graph and on a bar graph.
Home Activity: Together, graph information about your family, such as the number of minutes it takes to eat dinner each night for a week. Make both a circle and a bar graph.

© Scott Foresman 2

Name _____

T<u>ex</u>as

Write ex to finish each word.
Read each sentence.
Draw a line to match each sentence with its picture.

1. Let's go _____plore in this cave!   **a.**

2. Hallie wants to jump n _____ t.   **b.**

3. Phil is an _____pert biker.   **c.**

4. Alice has an _____tra cookie.   **d.**

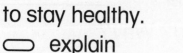

Find the word that matches each clue.
Mark the space to show your answer.

5. It's something you do to stay healthy.
   - ○ explain
   - ○ exercise
   - ○ explode

6. It's a way out of someplace.
   - ○ extra
   - ○ example
   - ○ exit

Notes for Home: Your child reviewed words with the vowel pattern *ex*, as in *Texas*. **Home Activity:** Write a list of words with *ex*, such as *explore, next, expensive,* or *exit*. Help your child read them aloud and use them in sentences.

174 **Phonics: Vowel Pattern *ex* Review**

Level 2.2

© Scott Foresman 2

| calf | half | laugh | phone | rough | tough |

Write three words from the box spelled with **gh**.

_____ _____ _____

1. _____ 2. _____ 3. _____

Write the word from the box that rhymes with  .

4. _____

Change one letter in each word to make a word from the box.
Write the new word on the line.

5. halt _____ 6. calm _____

Pick a word from the box to finish each sentence.
Write the word on the line.

sound
kept

7. I hear the _____ of popcorn popping.

8. Dean _____ it all for himself.

 Notes for Home: Your child spelled words with the consonants *gh, ph,* and *lf* and two frequently used words: *sound, kept.* **Home Activity:** Say each spelling word. Have your child use it in a sentence. Say the spelling word again, and have your child write it.

© Scott Foresman 2

Read the sentences Greg and Diane say to each other.
Follow the directions below.

Greg: What do we need to make lemonade?

Diane: We need lemons, sugar, water, and ice.

Diane: Stir it.

Greg: This is the best lemonade I've ever had!

---

1. Draw one line under the command.
2. Draw two lines under the exclamation.
3. Circle the question.
4. Put an X after the statement.
5. Look at the picture. Write a sentence that tells what happens next.

Notes for Home: Your child reviewed sentences. **Home Activity:** Read a story with your child. Ask him or her to identify different types of sentences (questions, statements, commands, and exclamations). Have your child read them aloud with the proper emotion.

© Scott Foresman 2

Part 1: Vocabulary

Find the word that best fits in each sentence.
Mark the space for your answer.

1. Write your name _____ the line.
   ○ ever   ○ above   ○ behind

2. The bird made a beautiful _____ .
   ○ sound   ○ number   ○ garbage

3. Jill _____ all her toys in a box.
   ○ began   ○ exclaimed   ○ kept

4. We have only a _____ cups of milk.
   ○ few   ○ whole   ○ enough

5. I like lots of _____ in my water.
   ○ paper   ○ ice   ○ room

© Scott Foresman 2

GO ON

Part 2: Comprehension

Read each question.
Mark the space for your answer.

6. The club members decided to make some money by —
   - ⬭ selling lemonade.
   - ⬭ having a bake sale.
   - ⬭ getting more members.

7. The kids wanted the money to —
   - ⬭ buy lemons.
   - ⬭ set up a corner stand.
   - ⬭ fix their clubhouse.

8. Few people got lemonade on Thursday because —
   - ⬭ the lemonade did not taste good.
   - ⬭ everyone went to watch Jed the juggler.
   - ⬭ Thursday's bar was way down low.

9. Sheri must have asked Jed to —
   - ⬭ do his act next to the lemonade stand.
   - ⬭ leave so they could sell more lemonade.
   - ⬭ never juggle again.

10. The Elm Street kids learned that —
    - ⬭ selling lemonade is no fun.
    - ⬭ they could not fix the clubhouse.
    - ⬭ a job is easier when everyone works together.

STOP

© Scott Foresman 2

disappear   dislike   remake   repaint   untie   unwrap

Pick a word from the box that is the opposite of each word below.
Write the word on the line.

1. tie

_____
- - - - - - - - - - - - - - - - - -
_____

2. wrap

_____
- - - - - - - - - - - - - - - - - -
_____

3. like

_____
- - - - - - - - - - - - - - - - - -
_____

4. appear

_____
- - - - - - - - - - - - - - - - - -
_____

Pick a word from the box that means the same as each group of words.
Write the word on the line.

5. paint again

_____
- - - - - - - - - - - - - - - - - -

6. make again

_____
- - - - - - - - - - - - - - - - - -

Find the word that matches each clue.
Mark the space to show your answer.

7. not lucky
- ⬭ unlucky
- ⬭ lucky
- ⬭ unkind

8. read again
- ⬭ understand
- ⬭ reread
- ⬭ return

Notes for Home: Your child reviewed words with the prefixes *un-*, *dis-*, and *re-*. **Home Activity:** Work with your child to write a list of words with the prefixes *un-*, *dis-*, and *re-*. Have your child read the words and illustrate their meanings.

© Scott Foresman 2

calf   half   laugh   phone   rough   tough

Pick a word from the box to match each picture.
Write the word on the line.

1.

_____
- - - - - - - - - - -

2.

_____
- - - - - - - - - - -

3.

_____
- - - - - - - - - - -

Unscramble the letters to make a word from the box.
Write the word on the line.

4. flha

_____
- - - - - - - - - - -

5. ogruh

_____
- - - - - - - - - - -

6. thugo

_____
- - - - - - - - - - -

Pick a word from the box to match each clue.
Write the word on the line.

sound   kept

_____
- - - - - - - - - - -

7. something you hear _____

_____
- - - - - - - - - - -

8. opposite of "gave away" _____

Notes for Home: Your child spelled words with the consonants *gh, ph,* and *lf* and two frequently used words: *sound, kept.* **Home Activity:** Have your child write sentences using the spelling words. Challenge your child to use words that rhyme.

© Scott Foresman 2

Family Times

Start Collecting! It's Fun!

The Puddle Pail

Keith's Leaves

My name is Keith.
I'll play outside today.
I'll collect some leaves
While I skip and play.

The leaves I'll collect
Are either green or brown.
I'll tape them to my ceiling
So they won't fall down.

I'll look at my leaves
While I lie in bed.
I'll put more leaves
On my shelves instead!

This rhyme includes words your child is working with in school: words with the long *e* sound spelled *ei* (*Keith*) and words in which *f* is changed to *v* before adding -*es* (*leaves, shelves*). Read aloud the rhyme with your child. Then write other plurals that change *f* to *v* before adding -*es*, such as *lives, knives,* and *wolves.*

(fold here)

Name: _____

© Scott Foresman 2

You are your child's first and best teacher!

Here are ways to help your child practice skills while having fun!

Day 1 Work with your child to write a list of long *e* words using *ei* such as *receive, either, Keith,* and *ceiling.* Read the words to your child and have him or her write them.

Day 2 Ask your child to write or say a funny story that uses any of the following words that your child is learning to read: *eight, road, round, start, young.*

Day 3 As you read together, ask your child to point out unfamiliar words. Encourage your child to use surrounding words and pictures to try to figure out the meaning of an unfamiliar word.

Day 4 Help your child write a letter to a friend or relative. Have your child address an envelope, put the letter in it, and take it to the post office or mailbox.

Day 5 Have your child write a story in which the characters speak. Have him or her use quotations marks as needed to show the speaker's exact words.

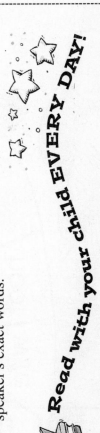

Read with your child EVERY DAY!

More Than One

Materials   1 coin, 1 button per player, game board

Game Directions

1. Players place buttons at Start.

2. Players take turns flipping a coin and moving 1 space for heads or 2 spaces for tails.

3. Each time a player lands on a word, he or she changes that word to show more than one. If the player misspells the word, the player goes back to the previous position.

4. The first player to reach the end wins!

Start
knife
scarf
leaf
life
loaf
half
calf
wolf
shelf
hoof
wife
End

Name _____

Start Collecting! It's Fun!
The Puddle Pail

Pick a word from the box to finish each sentence.
Write the word on the line.

| either | neither | receive | ceiling |

_____
– – – – – – – – – – – – – – – –
1. Did you _____ the two toy bugs I sent?

_____
– – – – – – – – – – – – – – – –
2. _____ one has come yet.

_____
– – – – – – – – – – – – – – – –
3. They may come _____ Friday or Saturday.

_____
– – – – – – – – – – – – – – – –
4. You can hang them from your _____ .

Notes for Home: Your child identified words with the long *e* sound spelled *ei* as in *ceiling*.
Home Activity: Work with your child to write sentences using the listed words.

© Scott Foresman 2

Name _____

Write the word for each picture.
Use the word in ( ) to help you.

leaf   lea**ves**

1.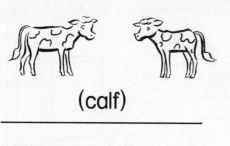

(calf)

_____

- - - - - - - - - - - - - - -

_____

2.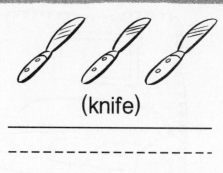

(knife)

_____

- - - - - - - - - - - - - - -

_____

3.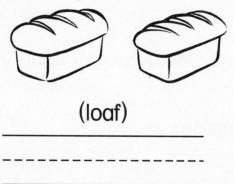

(loaf)

_____

- - - - - - - - - - - - - - -

_____

4.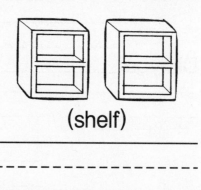

(shelf)

_____

- - - - - - - - - - - - - - -

_____

Draw a picture of the word below.

5. wolves

Notes for Home: Your child wrote plural words in which *f* is changed to *v* before adding
-es. **Home Activity:** Ask your child to write a sentence using each of the plural words above.

© Scott Foresman 2

Name _____

Read each sentence.
Circle the picture that shows the meaning
of the underlined word.

1. Al has a very <u>young</u> puppy.

2. Al and his puppy walk across the <u>road</u> to go to the park.

3. Al wants to <u>start</u> a rock collection.

4. Al found <u>eight</u> rocks.

5. This rock is very <u>round</u> and smooth.

Notes for Home: This week your child is learning to read the words *eight, road, round, start,* and *young.* **Home Activity:** Write these words on slips of paper and have your child practice reading them aloud and using them in sentences.

© Scott Foresman 2

Name _____

Start Collecting! It's Fun!
The Puddle Pail

Read each sentence.
Use the other words in the sentence and the pictures to help you figure out the meaning of the underlined word.
Circle the meaning of the word.

1. Carrie added a British pound to her collection.
   a. a kind of money or coin
   b. a scale

2. She likes to collect currency.
   a. type of food
   b. money

3. She stores her collection in a box.
   a. keeps
   b. shops

4. Carrie is eager to get more coins.
   a. not careful
   b. looking forward to

5. She adores collecting coins!
   a. decorates
   b. loves

Notes for Home: Your child used context clues—pictures or words that surround an unfamiliar word—to figure out a word's meaning. **Home Activity:** Read a story to your child. Ask him or her to use context clues to figure out the meanings of unfamiliar words.

© Scott Foresman 2

Name _____

Start Collecting! It's Fun!
The Puddle Pail

Quotation marks  " " show the beginning and
the end of what someone says.

Tim said, "Do you like my shells?"
"Yes, I do," Greta answered.

Put a ✓ on the line if the sentence does not need quotation marks.
Put an **X** on the line if the sentence needs quotation marks.
Then add quotation marks to the sentence.

_____

_____   **1.** Gus asked Nan to look at his baseball cards.
_____

_____   **2.** Nan said, You have a lot of cards.
_____

_____   **3.** Gus said, I've collected over 50 cards.
_____

_____   **4.** Nan asked her mom if she could collect cards too.
_____

_____   **5.** Her mom said, I'll help you get started.

Notes for Home: Your child identified sentences that use quotation marks. *Home Activity:*
Write a simple conversation between two characters or family members. Have your child help
you put the quotation marks where they belong.

© Scott Foresman 2

Pick a word from the box to match each clue.
Write the word on the line.

castle	crocodile	eight	puddle
road	round	shadows	young

1.

_____

– – – – – – – – –

2.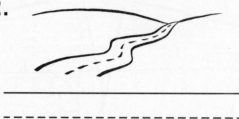

_____

– – – – – – – – –

3.

_____

– – – – – – – – –

4.

_____

– – – – – – – – –

5. They go everywhere you go!

_____

– – – – – – – – –

6. seven, _____, nine, ten

_____

– – – – – – – – –

7. not old, but _____

_____

– – – – – – – – –

8. A square is not, but a circle is.

_____

– – – – – – – – –

 Notes for Home: Your child matched clues with vocabulary words that he or she learned to read this week. *Home Activity:* Work with your child to write a story using as many of these words as possible.

© Scott Foresman 2

Name _____

monk**ey**   cook**ie**s

Circle the word for each picture.

1.	2.	3.	4.
piece peas	moan money	turkey turtle	honey hotter

5.	6.	7.	8.
keep key	donkey done	cheek chief	three thief

Find the word that has the same **long e** sound as the picture.
Mark the space to show your answer.

9. ⬭ veil
   ⬭ vase
   ⬭ valley

10. ⬭ felt
    ⬭ field
    ⬭ fried

Notes for Home: Your child reviewed words with long *e* spelled *ie* and *ey* as in *cookies* and *monkey*. **Home Activity:** Write a list of long *e* words spelled *ie* and *ey*. Have your child tell you a story using as many of the words as possible.

© Scott Foresman 2

| calves | halves | lives | leaves | shelves | wolves |

Write the word from the box that names more than one for each word below.

1. shelf _____

2. half _____

3. calf _____

4. leaf _____

5. life _____

6. wolf _____

Pick a word from the box to match each picture.
Write the word on the line.

7.

_____

8.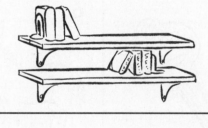

_____

Pick a word from the box to match each clue.
Write the word on the line.

| young | road |

9. not old

_____

10. rhymes with *toad*

_____

 Notes for Home: Your child spelled plural words that change *f* to *v* before adding *-es (calves)*, as well as two frequently used words: *young, road.* **Home Activity:** Write each spelling word on separate slips of paper. Take turns picking two words and using them both in a sentence.

© Scott Foresman 2

Read each sentence.
Add quotation marks if the sentence needs them.
Write an **X** after the sentence if quotation marks are not needed.

1. Cal wants to collect rocks.

2. He asks, Mom, can I have a bucket for my rocks?

3. His mom gives him a big bucket.

4. She says, Look in the backyard for rocks.

Add words to finish this sentence.
Write the complete sentence below.
Use quotation marks as needed.

5. Cal says, _____.

_____

- -

_____

- -

_____

Notes for Home: Your child identified sentences that require quotation marks and added them. ***Home Activity:*** Read a simple story with your child. Have him or her point out which sentences use quotation marks.

© Scott Foresman 2

Test-Taking Tips

1. Write your name on the test.

2. Read each question twice.

3. Read all the answer choices for the question.

4. Mark your answer carefully.

5. Check your answer.

© Scott Foresman 2

Name _____

Start Collecting! It's Fun!
The Puddle Pail

Part 1: Vocabulary

Find the word that best fits in each sentence.
Mark the space for your answer.

1. Hank made a picture with _____ stars.
   - ⬭ quite
   - ⬭ between
   - ⬭ eight

2. The _____ chick followed its mother.
   - ⬭ young
   - ⬭ whole
   - ⬭ near

3. The queen lived in a _____ .
   - ⬭ castle
   - ⬭ crocodile
   - ⬭ puddle

4. Which _____ goes to the lake?
   - ⬭ round
   - ⬭ road
   - ⬭ edge

5. The cat hides in the _____ .
   - ⬭ paws
   - ⬭ shadows
   - ⬭ attention

© Scott Foresman 2

GO ON ➤

Part 2: Comprehension

Read each question.
Mark the space for your answer.

6. Sol and Ernst first go to —
   - ⬭ a castle.
   - ⬭ the beach.
   - ⬭ the moon.

7. What does Ernst collect?
   - ⬭ puddles
   - ⬭ clouds
   - ⬭ feathers

8. You can tell from this story that starfishes are —
   - ⬭ cookies.
   - ⬭ animals.
   - ⬭ people.

9. How is Sol different from Ernst?
   - ⬭ Sol likes to eat blackberries.
   - ⬭ Sol is small and blue.
   - ⬭ Sol collects things he can keep.

10. The water in Ernst's pail is most like a —
    - ⬭ mirror.
    - ⬭ cloud.
    - ⬭ painting.

STOP

© Scott Foresman 2

Say the word for each picture.
Write gh, ph, or **lf** to finish each word.
Use the words in the box if you need help.

calf	cough	half
laugh	photos	trophy

ph̲one

1.

tro _____ y

2.

cou _____

3.

ha _____

4.

ca _____

5.

_____ otos

6.

lau _____

Pick the word that has the same ending sound as the picture.
Mark the space to show your answer.

7. ⊂⊃ rough
   ⊂⊃ rugs
   ⊂⊃ rush

8. ⊂⊃ thought
   ⊂⊃ tough
   ⊂⊃ tugs

Notes for Home: Your child reviewed words with the sound /f/ spelled *gh, ph,* and *lf (laugh, graph,* and *half).* **Home Activity:** Make a set of cards. Write words with the /f/ sound on half the cards. Illustrate the words on the other half. Have your child match the pairs of cards.

© Scott Foresman 2

calves	halves	lives	leaves	shelves	wolves

Pick a word from the box to match each clue.
Write the word on the line.

1. grows on trees

_____

2. more than one life

_____

3. like dogs

_____

4. baby cows

_____

5. where you find library books

_____

6. I half + I half = 2 _____

_____

Pick a word from the box to finish each sentence.
Write the word on the line.

young
road

7. The bus drives down the _____ .

8. It takes _____ children to school.

Notes for Home: Your child spelled plural words that change *f* to *v* before adding *-es* and two frequently used words: *young, road.* **Home Activity:** Help your child write sentences that use the spelling words. Together draw pictures to illustrate each sentence.

196 **Spelling: Plurals: Change *f* to *v* and Add *-es***

Level 2.2

© Scott Foresman 2

Family Times

Stone Soup

Stone Soup: A Folktale

The Country Fair

Let's go to the country fair.
We'll join the dairy contest.
A judge compares and then declares
Which cheese wedge tastes the very best.

Let's go to the country fair.
We saved up our bus fare.
We'll travel far and cross a bridge.
We'll bring our Swiss cheese to share.

This rhyme includes words your child is working with in school: words with *air* and *are (fair, fare)* and words with *dge (judge)*. Sing "The Country Fair" with your child. Together, find all the words with *air, are,* and *dge* in the rhyme.

(fold here)

Name: _____

© Scott Foresman 2

You are your child's first and best teacher!

Here are ways to help your child practice skills while having fun!

Day 1 Write *chair* and *spare* on two sheets of paper. Work with your child to write other words with *air* and *are* that rhyme with *chair* and *spare.*

Day 2 Ask your child to write or say sentences that use any of the following words that your child is learning to read: *add, any, both, making, mean.*

Day 3 After you read a story with your child, ask your child to tell you what happened in the beginning, middle, and end of the story.

Day 4 Have your child tell you about a movie, play, or TV show he or she has seen. Encourage your child to tell about the most important events in the movie, play, or TV show.

Day 5 Write a scene for a play about cooking food. Get family members to act out the different parts of the scene.

Read with your child EVERY DAY!

Cover It Up!

Materials 16 slips of paper, bag, 16 colored paper squares per player, game board

Game Directions

1. Write the 16 words shown below on slips of paper. Put the slips in a bag.

2. Each player cuts out small paper squares and colors them. Each player should use a different color for his or her set of squares.

3. Players take turns picking a slip of paper, reading the word aloud, and putting a colored paper square over the word on the gameboard.

4. The first player to cover 4 words in a row across, down, or diagonally wins!

Words
fair, hair, pair, prepare, stare, hare, dare, mare, airplane, hardware, care, fare, snare, chair, stair, spare

fair	hair	pair	prepare
stare	hare	dare	mare
airplane	hardware	care	fare
snare	chair	stair	spare

Name _____

Say the word for each picture.
Write air or **are** to finish each word.

st<u>are</u>

1.

h _____

2.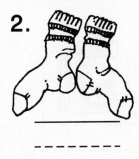

p _____

3.

sh _____

4.

h _____

5.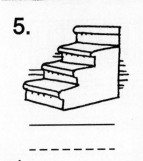

st _____ s

6.

m _____

7.

ch _____

8.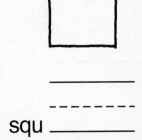

squ _____

Draw a picture for each word.

9. airplane

10. fair

Notes for Home: Your child identified words where the letter *r* changes the vowel sound of the word as in *chair* and *stare*. **Home Activity:** Work with your child to write silly sentences that rhyme using as many of the pictured words as possible.

© Scott Foresman 2

Name _____

Pick a word from the box to match each picture.
Write the word on the line.

badge	bridge	fudge	hedge	judge
ledge	pledge	smudge	wedge	

1.

_____

2.

_____

3.

_____

4.

_____

5.

_____

6.

_____

7.

_____

8.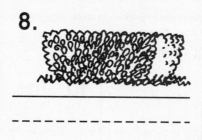

_____

9.

_____

Write a sentence using one of the words from the box.

10. _____

Notes for Home: Your child matched words with *dge* to pictures. **Home Activity:** Ask your child to read aloud the words in the box. Work together to write sentences that use these words.

© Scott Foresman 2

Name _____

Pick a word from the box to finish each sentence.
Write the word on the line.

add	any	both	making	mean

_____
1. What are you _____ ?

_____
2. Do you need _____ help?

_____
3. Please _____ the carrots.

_____
4. I think it needs _____ salt and pepper.

_____
5. What do you _____ ? I think it's too salty.

 Notes for Home: This week your child is learning to read the words *add, any, both, making,* and *mean.* **Home Activity:** Prepare a food item together. Before you start, write a list of the steps, using as many of these words as possible.

© Scott Foresman 2

Put the sentences in order to make a story.
Write 1, 2, 3, 4 on the lines to show the right order.

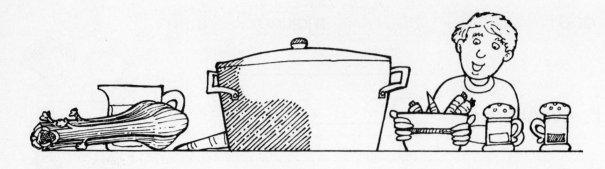

_____ 1. Danny wanted to make some soup.

_____ 2. Danny put the soup on the stove and cleaned up his mess.

_____ 3. He chopped up the vegetables and put them in the pot.

_____ 4. Danny got out a big pot, a spoon, and vegetables.

Draw a picture that shows something that happened in the middle of the story.

5.

Notes for Home: Your child identified the order of story events. **Home Activity:** Cut some short comic strips into separate panels. Ask your child to put them in their correct order. Ask your child to use the words *beginning, middle,* and *end* to describe what happens.

© Scott Foresman 2

Name _____

Here are some places where **commas** are used:

6 Morrow Court, Apt. 2B ◄——— **in addresses**
Salem, MA 01944

May 29, 2000 ◄——— **in dates**

Dear Harry, ◄——— **to start a letter**
How are you?
◄——— **to separate three or more things**
Liz, Jan, and Phil are going to the game next Saturday. Do you want to go with me?

Your friend, ◄——— **to end a letter**
Jimmy

I.–8. Add eight commas to this letter.

19 East Lake Dr.
Gladstone MI 49837

June 5 2000

Dear Uncle Sid

Sarah and I made soup for lunch. Sarah put carrots peas and mushrooms into a pot of water. I added salt pepper and garlic.

Love
Jake

Notes for Home: Your child placed commas in a letter. *Home Activity:* Together, write a postcard to a friend. Help your child place the commas in addresses, in dates, after the opening and closing, and when listing more than two items.

© Scott Foresman 2

Name _____

Pick a word from the box to match each clue.
Write the word on the line.

add	both	contest	delicious
judges	making	mean	stranger

1. something you enter to
   win a prize

   _____

2. We are _____ pies.

   _____

3. two together

   _____

4. people who choose
   the winner

   _____

5. a person you don't know

   _____

6. Did you _____ to call my
   cooking bad?

   _____

7. tastes great

   _____

8. join one thing to another

   _____

Notes for Home: Your child matched vocabulary words to clues. *Home Activity:* Write each
word on an index card. Take turns drawing a card, saying the word aloud, and using it in a
sentence.

© Scott Foresman 2

Name _____

Pick a **long e** word from the box to finish each sentence.
Write the word on the line.

> ceiling   either   Neil   receive

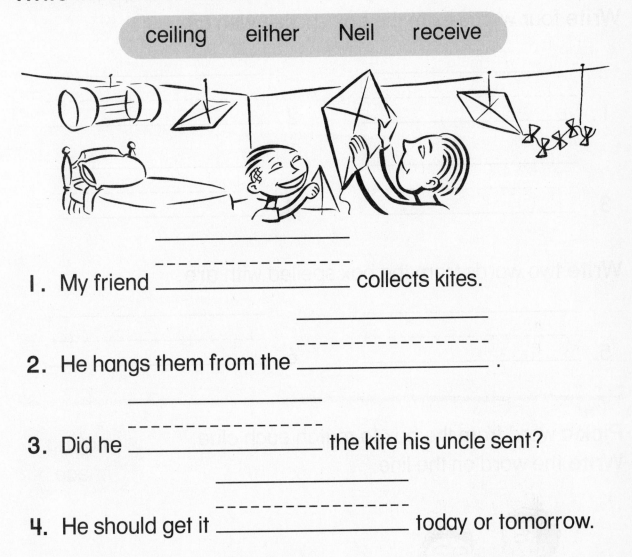

_____
- - - - - - - - - - - - - - -
1. My friend _____ collects kites.

_____
- - - - - - - - - - - - - - -
2. He hangs them from the _____ .

_____
- - - - - - - - - - - - - - -
3. Did he _____ the kite his uncle sent?

_____
- - - - - - - - - - - - - - -
4. He should get it _____ today or tomorrow.

Find the word that has the same **long e** sound as **receive**.
Mark the space to show your answer.

5. ⬭ seize
   ⬭ size
   ⬭ sister

6. ⬭ deck
   ⬭ dent
   ⬭ deceive

Notes for Home: Your child reviewed words with the long *e* sound spelled with *ei*, as in *ceiling*. **Home Activity:** Write a list of words with the long *e* sound spelled *ei* from this page. Have your child read them aloud to you.

© Scott Foresman 2

airplane   care   chair   hair   pair   share

Write four words from the box spelled with **air**.

1. _____   2. _____

3. _____   4. _____

Write two words from the box spelled with **are**.

5. _____   6. _____

Pick a word from the box to match each clue.
Write the word on the line.

making
mean

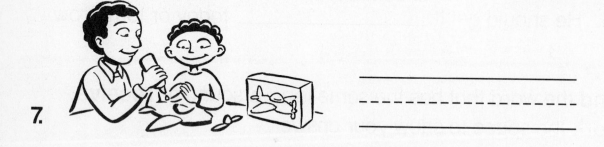

7. _____

8. Does this trophy _____ I won?

Notes for Home: Your child spelled words with *air* and *are,* such as *hair* and *share,* and two
frequently used words: *making, mean.* **Home Activity:** Write each spelling word, leaving
some spaces blank. (h_ _r; *hair*). Have your child fill in the missing letters.

© Scott Foresman 2

Level 2.2

Circle the commas.

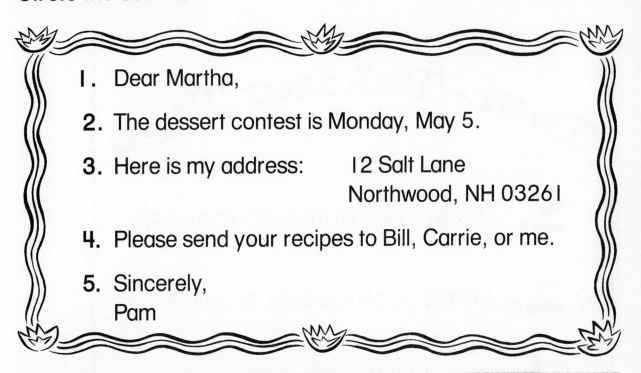

1. Dear Martha,

2. The dessert contest is Monday, May 5.

3. Here is my address: 12 Salt Lane
                            Northwood, NH 03261

4. Please send your recipes to Bill, Carrie, or me.

5. Sincerely,
   Pam

Write the commas where they belong.

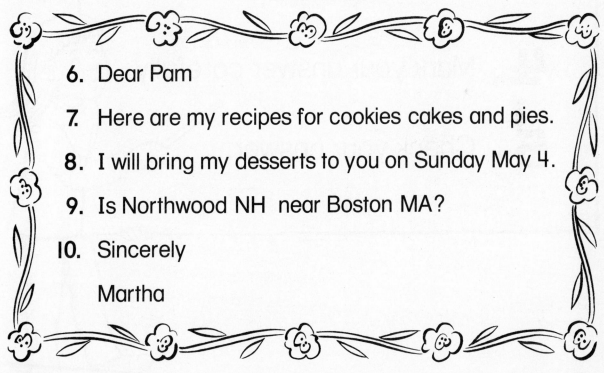

6. Dear Pam

7. Here are my recipes for cookies cakes and pies.

8. I will bring my desserts to you on Sunday May 4.

9. Is Northwood NH near Boston MA?

10. Sincerely

    Martha

Notes for Home: Your child identified and placed commas. *Home Activity:* Together, write postcards to a real or imaginary pen pal. Have your child point out where commas should be placed.

© Scott Foresman 2

Test-Taking Tips

1. Write your name on the test.

2. Read each question twice.

3. Read all the answer choices for the question.

4. Mark your answer carefully.

5. Check your answer.

© Scott Foresman 2

Part 1: Vocabulary

Find the word that best fits in each sentence.
Mark the space for your answer.

1. Holly loves _____ cookies.
   - ⬭ making
   - ⬭ sealing
   - ⬭ dashing

2. Julio won the baking _____ .
   - ⬭ contest
   - ⬭ stranger
   - ⬭ deck

3. They _____ like to paint.
   - ⬭ mean
   - ⬭ both
   - ⬭ add

4. The _____ say my soup is the best.
   - ⬭ Earth
   - ⬭ spiders
   - ⬭ judges

5. What a _____ cake!
   - ⬭ few
   - ⬭ delicious
   - ⬭ young

© Scott Foresman 2

GO ON ➡

Part 2: Comprehension

Read each question.
Mark the space for your answer.

6. The person who wins the contest gets a —
   ⬯ bowl of soup.
   ⬯ gold soup ladle.
   ⬯ black pot.

7. Who are the judges in the contest?
   ⬯ Minnie Stronie and Ann Chovie
   ⬯ Vida Minn and Ida Know
   ⬯ Brock Lee and Sal Lamie

8. The judges had second helpings of Ida Know's soup because they —
   ⬯ really liked it.
   ⬯ were very hungry.
   ⬯ did not know what was in it.

9. Which sentence tells about Bill Lownie?
   ⬯ He likes to eat soup.
   ⬯ He does not know how to cook.
   ⬯ He likes to play tricks.

10. Which could **not** really happen?
   ⬯ having a soup contest
   ⬯ making good soup from only a stone
   ⬯ living in a town called Bellie Acres

STOP

© Scott Foresman 2

Name _____

 leaf

leaves

Draw a picture for each word.

---

1. wolf

2. shelf

---

3. calves

4. wolves

---

5. shelves

6. calf

Find the word that matches each picture.
Mark the space to show your answer.

7. ⬭ scars
   ⬭ scarf
   ⬭ scarves

8. ⬭ loaf
   ⬭ loans
   ⬭ loaves

 Notes for Home: Your child reviewed words that change *f* to *v* and add *-es* to mean more than one. **Home Activity:** Write a list of singular words such as *half, calf, knife, loaf, shelf,* and *wolf.* Have your child write the plural spelling for each word.

© Scott Foresman 2

| airplane | care | chair | hair | pair | share |

Change one letter of each word to make a word from the box.
Write the word on the line.

1. chain

_____
- - - - - - - - - - - - - - - - - - -
_____

2. pail

_____
- - - - - - - - - - - - - - - - - - -
_____

3. shore

_____
- - - - - - - - - - - - - - - - - - -
_____

4. cart

_____
- - - - - - - - - - - - - - - - - - -
_____

Pick a word from the box to match each clue.
Write the word on the line.

5. something a pilot flies

_____
- - - - - - - - - - - - - - - - - - -
_____

6. grows on your head

_____
- - - - - - - - - - - - - - - - - - -
_____

Pick a word from the box to finish each rhyme.
Write the word on the line.

making
mean

_____
- - - - - - - - - - - - - - - - -

7. What do you _____?
That frog isn't green!

_____
- - - - - - - - - - - - - - - - - - -

8. Is it a pie you are _____?
Or a cake you are baking?

Notes for Home: Your child spelled words with *air* and *are,* such as *hair* and *share,* and two
frequently used words: *making, mean.* **Home Activity:** Mix up the letters of each spelling
word. Have your child unscramble and spell each word correctly.

© Scott Foresman 2

Level 2.2

Family Times

A Good Idea

Annie's Gifts

The School Chorus

I like singing in the chorus
And when there's a school play.
We will sing a chord or two
And practice every Friday.

I will use a microphone
Singing with my classmates.
We will wear our uniforms.
Our chorus sounds just first-rate!

Later on we'll have some treats
Like bagels and some cocoa.
Before we eat the band will play
And I will play the oboe.

I will use a microphone . . .

This rhyme includes words your child is working with in school: words with long vowels at the end of syllables *(microphone, uniform)* and the consonants *ch* and *sch (chorus, school)*. Sing "The School Chorus" with your child. Take turns singing a line and then having the other person repeat the same line.

(fold here)

Name: _____

© Scott Foresman 2

You are your child's first and best teacher!

Here are ways to help your child practice skills while having fun!

Day 1 Write the words *anchor, chorus, ache,* and *stomach.* Have your child read each word aloud and listen for the sound /k/ that the letters *ch* represent. Have your child compare this sound to the sound *ch* stands for in *chair, lunch,* and *chicken.*

Day 2 Write simple sentences that use any of the following words that your child is learning to read: *also, group, soon, though, tried.* Have your child read each sentence aloud.

Day 3 After reading a story, ask your child questions about its theme, such as: *What lessons did the characters learn? Are these lessons something you can use in your life?*

Day 4 Ask your child to write about a book he or she has read. Encourage your child to include what he or she likes about the book and why it would be interesting to other people.

Day 5 Look through some favorite stories with your child. Point out commas in sentences and discuss why commas are used.

Read with your child EVERY DAY!

Read for Points

Materials index cards, markers, timer

Game Directions

1. Write the words shown on page 3 on index cards.

2. Divide the cards among 2 or 4 players.

3. Players take turns choosing a card from another player's hand. If the first player is able to read the word and use it in a sentence, he or she earns 1 point. If not, the player returns the card to the original player's hand.

4. Play until all cards have been used. The player with the most points at the end wins! If the score is tied, take 1 minute to write as many two-syllable words as possible. Then the player with most words wins!

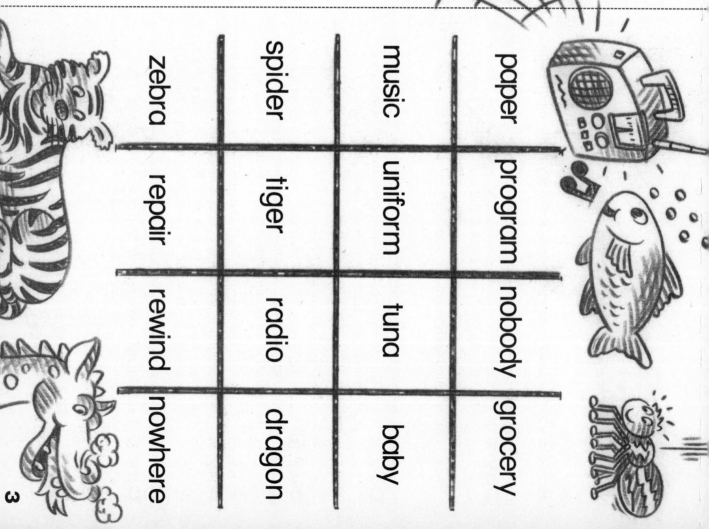

paper	program	nobody	grocery
music	uniform	tuna	baby
spider	tiger	radio	dragon
zebra	repair	rewind	nowhere

Say the word for each picture.
Write a, e, i, o, or **u** on the line to finish the word.

tom**a**t**o**

1.

r _____ dio

2.

z _____ bra

3.

comp _____ ter

4.

m _____ sic

5.

p _____ lot

6.

b _____ by

7.

t _____ ger

8.

m _____ tor

Notes for Home: Your child completed words with long vowel sounds at the end of syllables as in *to•ma•to*. **Home Activity:** Write these words: *navy, lazy, zebra, tiny, lion, total, October, tuba.* Help your child say each word and identify the long vowel sounds.

© Scott Foresman 2

Circle the word for each picture.

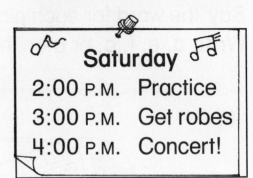

Saturday
2:00 P.M.   Practice
3:00 P.M.   Get robes
4:00 P.M.   Concert!

choir's **sch**edule

1.

chorus   chore

2.

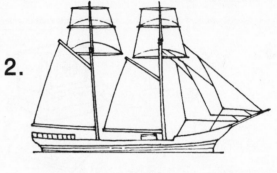

sooner   schooner

3.

school   stool

4.

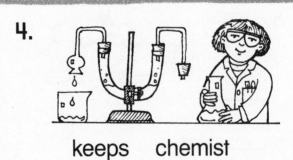

keeps   chemist

5.

ankle   anchor

6.

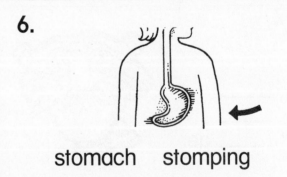

stomach   stomping

Notes for Home: Your child identified words with the consonants *ch* and *sch* that represent the sounds /k/ and /sk/ respectively. **Home Activity:** Help your child use these words in sentences.

Level 2.2

© Scott Foresman 2

Pick a word from the box to finish each sentence.
Write the word on the line.

| also | group | soon | though | tried |

1. Lil saw this _____ play.

2. When she got home, she _____ to play too.

3. Her little brother Kevin _____ tried to play.

4. Even _____ he is little, Kevin is a good partner.

5. They both will take piano lessons _____ .

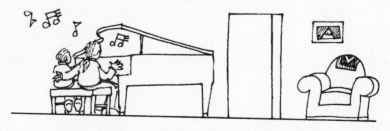

Notes for Home: This week your child is learning to read the words *also, group, soon, though,* and *tried.* **Home Activity:** Have your child tell a story using as many of the words as possible.

© Scott Foresman 2

Name _____

Read the story.
Follow the directions below.

Max wanted to be in a club. He tried out for the school play. But he didn't get a part. Max thought about joining the school chorus. But he sounds like a frog when he sings.

Max was sad. His mom told him to keep trying because everyone is good at something.

One day, Max saw the soccer club playing soccer. He liked sports. Maybe he would like soccer. Max joined the game. He was surprised when he scored a goal. The other players asked Max to play with them every afternoon. Max was happy to say "Yes!"

1. Underline the sentence that tells the story's big idea.
2. Write a sentence that tells what you learned from the story.

_____
- -
_____
_____
- -
_____

Draw two pictures. One should show how Max felt at the beginning of the story, and one should show how he felt at the end.

3.   4.

Notes for Home: Your child identified the theme of a story. *Home Activity:* Read a story to your child. Discuss the theme. Ask your child to tell you what the big idea is in the story and to share anything he or she learned from the story.

© Scott Foresman 2

Commas are placed between the date and the year.
They also go between the day of the week and the date.

Hannah was born on May 5, 1991.
She will have a party on Saturday, May 3.

Commas are also used to join two complete sentences with a connecting word like *and*.

Harry likes to play the drums, and he likes to sing.

Read each sentence.
Add commas where they are missing.

1. The play is on June 26 2000.

2. Tryouts will begin Sunday April 5.

3. They will start to practice on Tuesday April 7.

4. Everyone got a part so all the children were happy.

5. The play was great and everyone wants to do it again!

Notes for Home: Your child added commas to dates and compound sentences. *Home Activity:* Read a story with your child. Ask your child to point out the commas in the sentences. Talk about why these commas are used where they are.

© Scott Foresman 2

Draw a line to match each word on the left to a clue on the right.

| also | group | instrument | radio |
| soon | squeaked | though | tried |

1. also

    a. a mouse might have done this

2. group

    b.

3. instrument

    c. too

4. radio

    d. made an effort

5. soon

    e.

6. squeaked

    f.

7. though

    g. in a short while

8. tried

    h. She spoke up, even _____ she was shy.

Notes for Home: Your child matched the words above with word and picture clues. **Home Activity:** Work with your child to tell a story using as many of these words as possible. Take turns, each person adding one sentence to the story at a time.

© Scott Foresman 2

h<u>are</u>      ch<u>air</u>

Say the word for each picture.
Write air or **are** to finish each word.

1.	**2.**	**3.**	**4.**
p _____	st _____ s	c _____	st _____

5.	**6.**	**7.**	**8.**
squ _____	f _____	h _____	_____ plane

Find the word that has the same vowel sound as **chair**.
Mark the space to show your answer.

9. ⬭ dare
   ⬭ dark
   ⬭ drain

10. ⬭ sprain
    ⬭ spark
    ⬭ spare

Notes for Home: Your child reviewed words with *air* and *are* where the letter *r* changes the vowel sounds, such as *hare* and *chair*. **Home Activity:** Challenge your child to make up sentences that rhyme using the words on this page. *(There's a hare on the chair!)*

© Scott Foresman 2

| ache | chord | chorus | echo | school | stomach |

Unscramble the letters to make a word from the box.
Write the word on the line.

1. msocaht

_____

- - - - - - - - - - - - - - -

_____

2. rucosh

_____

- - - - - - - - - - - - - - -

_____

3. haec

_____

- - - - - - - - - - - - - - -

_____

4. coeh

_____

- - - - - - - - - - - - - - -

_____

Write the word from the box that rhymes with each word below.

_____

- - - - - - - - - - - - - -

5. cool _____

_____

- - - - - - - - - - - - - -

6. board _____

Pick a word from the box to finish each sentence.
Write the word on the line.

though
group

_____

- - - - - - - - - - - - - - - - - -

7. Jill plays flute for a small _____ of people.

_____

- - - - - - - - - - - - - -

8. Even _____ it is late, Jill keeps playing.

Notes for Home: Your child spelled words with the sounds /k/ spelled *ch* as in *chorus* and /sk/ spelled *sch* as in *school* and two frequently used words: *though, group*. **Home Activity:** Say each spelling word. Have your child use it in a sentence. Then have your child write each word.

© Scott Foresman 2

Read each sentence.

Circle the comma in each sentence.

1. Jill likes to play the drums, and Ben likes to sing.

2. Phil likes to draw, but Tammy does not.

3. Molly plays soccer, and Tommy cheers for her.

4. Sam wanted to be in the play, but he missed the tryouts.

5. Karen joined the math club, and she won a trophy.

Read each sentence.

Add a comma where it belongs in each sentence.

6. Liz takes flute lessons but she doesn't enjoy them.

7. Her mom wants her to practice but Liz likes to play outdoors.

8. Liz drew a picture of herself playing baseball and she gave it to her mom.

9. Her mom had an idea and she took Liz to baseball tryouts.

10. Liz joined the baseball team and she is much happier.

Notes for Home: Your child identified and placed commas in compound sentences—two complete sentences joined by a comma and a connecting word like *and* or *but*. **Home Activity:** Read a simple news article with your child. Look for compound sentences.

© Scott Foresman 2

Test-Taking Tips

1. Write your name on the test.

2. Read each question twice.

3. Read all the answer choices
for the question.

4. Mark your answer carefully.

5. Check your answer.

© Scott Foresman 2

Part I: Vocabulary

Find the word that best fits in each sentence.

Mark the space for your answer.

1. Ed went to school, and I went _____ .
   ⊂⊃ friend   ⊂⊃ also   ⊂⊃ thumb

2. Anya _____ to read her brother's book.
   ⊂⊃ tried   ⊂⊃ squeaked   ⊂⊃ exclaimed

3. A _____ of children marched down the street.
   ⊂⊃ spray   ⊂⊃ group   ⊂⊃ patch

4. Jack eats peas even _____ he doesn't really like them.
   ⊂⊃ until   ⊂⊃ both   ⊂⊃ though

5. Please turn off the _____ .
   ⊂⊃ garbage   ⊂⊃ homework   ⊂⊃ radio

GO ON ➡

© Scott Foresman 2

Part 2: Comprehension

Read each question.
Mark the space for your answer.

6. Who played in the school band?
   - ⬭ Patty
   - ⬭ Lee
   - ⬭ Annie

7. What did Annie try to play last?
   - ⬭ drums
   - ⬭ recorder
   - ⬭ piano

8. How did Annie feel after she sang for the guests?
   - ⬭ sad
   - ⬭ excited
   - ⬭ happy

9. What did Annie learn in this story?
   - ⬭ Music is the best thing in the world.
   - ⬭ Most people don't try hard enough.
   - ⬭ Everyone has special gifts.

10. Which one did **not** really happen in the story?
    - ⬭ Frogs jumped in the house.
    - ⬭ Daddy and Momma danced at night.
    - ⬭ Annie drew some pictures.

© Scott Foresman 2

Circle the word for each picture. ba**dge**

1.

ledge   leave

2.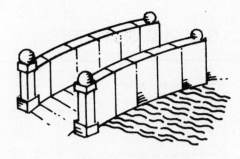

bridge   bring

3.

fudge   funnel

4.

jug   judge

Find the word that has the same ending sound as **badge**.
Mark the space to show your answer.

5. ⬭ edge
   ⬭ egg
   ⬭ end

6. ⬭ plug
   ⬭ plaid
   ⬭ pledge

 Notes for Home: Your child reviewed the sound /j/ spelled *dge* as in *badge*. **Home Activity:** Challenge your child to use the words with *dge* listed above in sentences. Work together to illustrate each sentence.

© Scott Foresman 2

| ache | chord | chorus | echo | school | stomach |

Pick a word from the box to match each clue.
Write the word on the line.

I. a group of singers
_____
- - - - - - - - - - - - - - - - - - -
_____

2. where your food goes
_____
- - - - - - - - - - - - - - - - - - -
_____

3. a place to learn
_____
- - - - - - - - - - - - - - - - - - -
_____

4. a hurt
_____
- - - - - - - - - - - - - - - - - - -
_____

5. rhymes with *sword*
_____
- - - - - - - - - - - - - - - - - - -
_____

6. a sound you hear again
_____
- - - - - - - - - - - - - - - - - - -
_____

Pick a word from the box to finish each sentence.
Write the word on the line.

though
group

7. _____ Tim likes tennis, he likes baseball more.
- - - - - - - - - - - - - - -

8. Tim likes to play with a _____ of people.
- - - - - - - - - - - - - - - - - -

Notes for Home: Your child spelled words with the consonant sound /k/ spelled *ch* and two
frequently used words: *though, group.* **Home Activity:** Have your child write the spelling
words on paper. Cut and mix the letters. Have your child use the letters to rebuild the words.

© Scott Foresman 2

Family Times

Wicker School Takes Action

City Green

Have You Heard?

Have you heard about our great plan?
We'll help our town and learn.
We'll wake up at an early hour.
Pride is what we'll earn.

It's our vacation. We have time.
We'll take some action now.
It is tradition to help out.
Just watch. We'll show you how.

We'll search our streets and look for trash
On our spring vacation.
We'll set in motion our great plans.
We'll have a celebration.

This rhyme includes words your child is working with in school: words with *ear* and *our* in which the letter *r* changes the vowel sound (*early, hour*) and words with the syllable pattern -*tion* (*action*). Read aloud "Have You Heard?" with your child. Clap every time you say a word that ends in -*tion*.

(fold here)

Name: _____

© Scott Foresman 2

You are your child's first and best teacher!

Here are ways to help your child practice skills while having fun!

Day 1 Your child is working with the syllable pattern -*tion* as in *nation, motion,* and *action.* Look through a newspaper together and circle words with -*tion.*

Day 2 Ask your child to write sentences that rhyme and include these words: *already; buy; nothing, piece,* and *used.*

Day 3 Watch a TV show with your child. Have your child make judgments about characters' actions. Ask questions such as: *Was that a smart thing to do? Is that what you would do?*

Day 4 Look at some letters to the editor in a newspaper. Ask your child to write a letter trying to persuade readers about the need to help improve the neighborhood.

Day 5 Talk with your child about how he or she would present information to a group of younger children, to a group of children his or her own age, and to a group of adults. Discuss how you might change how you speak depending on your audience.

Read with your child EVERY DAY!

Finish the Word!

Materials 1 coin, 1 button per player, game board

Game Directions

1. Players place their buttons on Start.

2. Players take turns flipping a coin and moving one space for heads or two spaces for tails.

3. Players add *ear* or *our* to the letters in each space on the gameboard to finish the words. A player then uses the word in a sentence. If a player cannot finish the word or use it correctly in a sentence, the player moves back to his or her previous position.

4. The first player to reach the end wins!

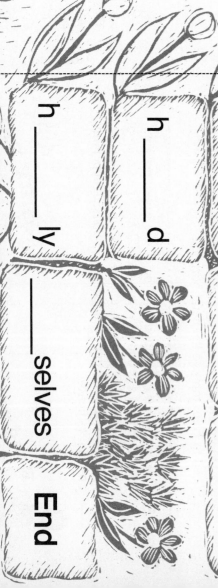

Start

___ ly

p ___ l

s ___

n l ___ n

n ___

s ___ ch

fl ___

h ___ n

h ___ d

h ___ ly

___ selves

End

Read the word at the top of each column.
Write the words from the box that have the same vowel sound.

flour   Earth   heard   pearls   sour

early

1. _____

2. _____

3. _____

hour

4. _____

5. _____

Pick a word from the box to match each clue.
Write the word on the line.

6.

_____

7.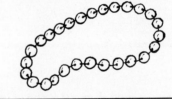

_____

8. It sounds the same as *flower*.

_____

9. not sweet, but _____

_____

10. _____

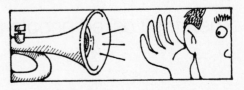

Notes for Home: Your child read and wrote words where the letter *r* changes the vowel sound as in *(heard, sour)*. **Home Activity:** Ask your child to write and then read a sentence using each of the following words: *earn, search, hour, sour.*

© Scott Foresman 2

Circle a word to finish each sentence.

1. The stream near the school was full of _____.

   pollution
   pollute

2. The children wanted to take _____ to clean it up.

   acting
   action

3. They held a clean-up day during their _____.

   vacation
   vacate

4. They spent the day _____ garbage.

   collecting
   collection

5. Then they asked people to sign a _____ .

   petting
   petition

Notes for Home: Your child read words that include the syllable *-tion* as in *lotion.* **Home**
Activity: Write or say words with *-tion (attention, solution, prediction, fiction, creation).* Give
your child clues about the word to help him or her guess the meaning.

© Scott Foresman 2

Name _____

Read each sentence.
Circle the picture that shows the meaning for
each underlined word.

1. Beth picked an empty <u>piece</u> of the garden to use.

2. Dave went to <u>buy</u> some seeds.

3. Beth and Dave <u>used</u> tools to dig a hole in the soil.

4. At first, <u>nothing</u> grew.

 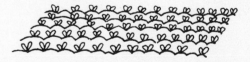

5. Now, only a week later, the plants have <u>already</u> sprouted.

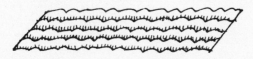 

 Notes for Home: This week your child is learning to read the words *already, buy, nothing, piece,* and *used.* **Home Activity:** Have your child write or tell a story about working together using these words.

© Scott Foresman 2

Name _____

Read each sentence.

Write H if the person is doing something helpful.

Write N if the person is doing something that is **not** helpful.

_____

_____ 1. Tommy threw his wrapper on the ground.

_____

_____ 2. Sue collected money to buy a new slide.

_____

_____ 3. Tal used the money to buy himself a snack.

_____

_____ 4. Jason fixed the broken swing.

Draw a picture to show something helpful that one of the children did.

5.

Notes for Home: Your child made judgments about actions that are helpful and those that are not. **Home Activity:** As you read, ask your child whether the characters are acting in a good way or a bad way. Ask your child why he or she thinks a particular action is good or bad.

© Scott Foresman 2

Level 2.2

Name _____

Circle the sentences that tell about the same idea.
Put these sentences in order to make a paragraph.
Write numbers in front of these sentences to show the order.

_____ 1. The children waited for the plants to grow.

_____ 2. It was time to plant a garden.

_____ 3. Chris and Tina went for a walk.

_____ 4. Chris planted the seeds and watered them.

_____ 5. Tim played football in the park.

_____ 6. We went to visit Grandma.

_____ 7. Spring had come.

_____ 8. Everyone had a job to do.

Notes for Home: Your child identified sentences that can be grouped into a paragraph.
Home Activity: Have your child write sentences about a time he or she did something as part
of the neighborhood or community. Help your child put the sentences into paragraphs.

© Scott Foresman 2

Name _____

Pick a word from the box to match each clue.
Write the word on the line.

already	buy	empty	nothing
piece	property	soil	used

1. not full

   _____
   - - - - - - - - - - - - -
   _____

2. She _____ a shovel to dig.

   _____
   - - - - - - - - - - - - -
   _____

3. I _____ planted my garden.

   _____
   - - - - - - - - - - - - -
   _____

4. dirt

   _____
   - - - - - - - - - - - - -
   _____

5.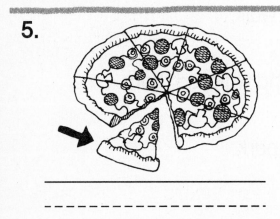

   _____
   - - - - - - - - - - - - -
   _____

6.

   _____
   - - - - - - - - - - - - -
   _____

7. the opposite of *everything*

   _____
   - - - - - - - - - - - - -
   _____

8. something you own

   _____
   - - - - - - - - - - - - -
   _____

Notes for Home: Your child completed sentences using words that he or she learned to read this week. *Home Activity:* Play act that you and your child are planting a garden. Try to use as many words from the list above as you can.

© Scott Foresman 2

Say the word for the picture.

Write a, e, i, o, or **u** to finish each word.

t<u>i</u>ger

1.
p ____ pers

2.
b ____ cycle

3.
p ____ ny

4.
p ____ tatoes

5.
l ____ on

6.
____ pron

7.
r ____ ler

8.
z ____ bra

Find the missing long vowel sound in each word.

Mark the space to show your answer.

9. phot ___
◯ a ◯ u ◯ o

10. tr ___ angle
◯ a ◯ i ◯ e

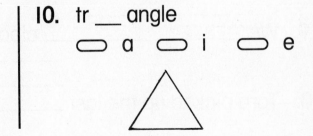

Notes for Home: Your child reviewed words with long vowels at the end of syllables as in *tiger*. **Home Activity:** Work with your child to make picture cards with word labels of the words on this page. Have your child pick a card, read the word aloud, and use it in a sentence.

© Scott Foresman 2

Name _____

| earn | flour | heard | hour | learn | sour |

Write three words from the box spelled with **ear**.

1. _____ 2. _____ 3. _____

Write three words from the box spelled with **our**.

4. _____ 5. _____ 6. _____

Write two words from the box that rhyme with **burn**.

7. _____ 8. _____

Pick a word from the box to finish each sentence.
Write the word on the line.

piece
already

9. We _____ cleaned up the playground.

10. Tara picked up the last _____ of trash.

Notes for Home: Your child spelled words with the *r*-controlled vowels *ear* and *our* in which the letter *r* changes the sound of the vowel, as well as two frequently used words: *piece, already*. **Home Activity:** Help your child use these words to write a short story.

© Scott Foresman 2

Name _____

Leave out details that do **not** support the main idea.

Main Idea: We need to clean the park.
John will pick up trash.
~~Pat will go for a bike ride~~.

Read the sentence that tells the main idea.
Cross out the sentence that does **not** support the main idea.

1. **Main Idea:** Our city needs a skateboard park.
   Many people enjoy using skateboards.
   Skateboards don't cost very much.
   It isn't safe to skateboard in the streets.

2. **Main Idea:** Do something besides watching TV.
   There are too many ads on TV.
   You can make something with your hands.
   You can play make-believe with a friend.

3. **Main Idea:** Dogs are smart animals.
   Dogs can understand commands.
   Some dogs have long hair.
   A dog remembers what you teach it.

Write a sentence to go with this main idea:

4. A cow does not make a very good pet.

_____

_ _

_____

Notes for Home: Your child identified sentences that did not belong with the main idea of a paragraph. *Home Activity:* Have your child give you a main idea. Make up sentences that go with it and one that does not. Ask your child which sentence does not belong. Switch roles.

© Scott Foresman 2

Name _____

Read the paragraph.
Underline a sentence if it belongs in the paragraph.
Draw a line through it if it does **not** belong in the paragraph.

1.–8.   Jess wants to plant a garden.
Jess picks a spot for the garden.
She dusts the shelves.
She digs in the dirt.
She plants the seeds.
Jess brushes her hair.
She waters her seeds.
Jess loves to read books.

Add two sentences of your own to finish the paragraph.

9. _____

_____

10. _____

_____

Notes for Home: Your child identified sentences that can be grouped into a paragraph.
Home Activity: Help your child write a story. Work together to group the sentences
together into paragraphs.

© Scott Foresman 2

Part 1: Vocabulary

Find the word that best fits in each sentence.
Mark the space for your answer.

1. I need a _____ of tape.
   - ⊂⊃ word
   - ⊂⊃ piece
   - ⊂⊃ number

2. The cookie jar is _____ again.
   - ⊂⊃ empty
   - ⊂⊃ nothing
   - ⊂⊃ calm

3. Are you done _____ ?
   - ⊂⊃ between
   - ⊂⊃ never
   - ⊂⊃ already

4. The Changs bought a _____ car.
   - ⊂⊃ used
   - ⊂⊃ round
   - ⊂⊃ pleased

5. We planted the seeds in the _____ .
   - ⊂⊃ tool
   - ⊂⊃ wheel
   - ⊂⊃ soil

© Scott Foresman 2

GO ON ➡

Part 2: Comprehension

Read each question.
Mark the space for your answer.

6. The building was torn down because it was —
   - ☐ ugly.
   - ☐ new.
   - ☐ unsafe.

7. How did Old Man Hammer feel when he looked at the empty lot?
   - ☐ pleased
   - ☐ upset
   - ☐ excited

8. What did the neighbors do first?
   - ☐ They paid one dollar to rent the lot.
   - ☐ They planted seeds.
   - ☐ They cleaned up the junk.

9. The neighbors work together to —
   - ☐ knock down the building.
   - ☐ make something good.
   - ☐ buy the empty lot.

10. Who worked the most to make the garden?
    - ☐ Old Man Hammer
    - ☐ Marcy
    - ☐ Mr. Bennett

STOP

© Scott Foresman 2

Say the word for each picture.
Write ch or **sch** to finish each word.

an**ch**or

1. _____ **ool**

2. _____ **orus**

3. stoma _____

4. e _____ o

Find the word where **ch** has the same sound heard in **anchor**.
Mark the space to show your answer.

5. ⬭ lunch
⬭ chair
⬭ ache

6. ⬭ character
⬭ branches
⬭ chin

Notes for Home: Your child reviewed the consonant sounds /k/ spelled *ch* (*chorus*) and /sk/ spelled *sch* (*school*). **Home Activity:** Write each word from this page on an index card. Place them around a room. When your child finds a card, have him or her read the word to you.

© Scott Foresman 2

earn   flour   heard   hour   learn   sour

Write a word from the box to match each picture.

1.

_____

- - - - - - - - - - - - - - - -

_____

2.

_____

- - - - - - - - - - - - - - - -

_____

3.

_____

- - - - - - - - - - - - - - - -

_____

4.

_____

- - - - - - - - - - - - - - - -

_____

5.

_____

- - - - - - - - - - - - - - - -

_____

6.

_____

- - - - - - - - - - - - - - - -

_____

Pick a word from the box to match each clue.
Write the word on the line.

piece   already

7. rhymes with *steady*

_____

- - - - - - - - - - - - - - - -

8. a part of something

_____

- - - - - - - - - - - - - - - -

Notes for Home: Your child spelled words with *r*-controlled vowels *ear* and *our* where the letter *r* changes the vowel sound and two frequently used words: *piece, already.* **Home Activity:** Help your child write and illustrate a short story that uses the spelling words.

© Scott Foresman 2

Correct each sentence.
Write it on the line.
Hint: Use capital letters and the correct end marks.

1. i help mrs. woo

_____

_____

2. how do you help her

_____

_____

3. we pick up trash in oak park

_____

_____

_____

4. a clean park is nice

_____

_____

5. flowers grow there in may

_____

_____

Notes for Home: Your child capitalized the beginning of sentences and proper nouns and wrote end marks for sentences. **_Home Activity:_** Write sentences for your child to check. Have him or her tell you if the sentences are written correctly.

© Scott Foresman 2

Words I Can Now Read and Write

_____   _____

_____   _____

_____   _____

_____   _____

_____   _____

_____

© Scott Foresman 2

© Scott Foresman 2

Name _____

Reading Log

Date	What is the title?	Who is the author?	What did you think of it?

Name _____

Reading Log

Date	What is the title?	Who is the author?	What did you think of it?

© Scott Foresman 2

© Scott Foresman 2

Name _____

Reading Log

Date	What is the title?	Who is the author?	What did you think of it?

Name _____

Reading Log

Date	What is the title?	Who is the author?	What did you think of it?

© Scott Foresman 2